SELAH:
Coffee with God

ANNA DOUBBLESTEIN

ISBN 978-1-0980-3699-7 (paperback)
ISBN 978-1-0980-3700-0 (digital)

Christian Faith Publishing, Inc.
832 Park Avenue
Meadville, PA 16335
www.christianfaithpublishing.com

Printed in the United States of America

To Sharon Martin, for loving me with and without my disability and for waiting patiently for me to finish this book. To Laura Napora, who never makes me feel disabled at all.

CONTENTS

INTRODUCTION

I wrote this book, I typed it out with only two fingers. I made this book not only easy to read and a lot of scripture, so you will not have to go back and forth between your Bible and this book. I do not know about your injury, but with mine, it is hard to handle books. I talk about the hard and unpopular things in this book we, with disability, or a caregiver thinks about. Things such as when God says no, what we all go through, having a disability or caring for a loved one with a disability. I had no pain at all writing a book and had plenty of time. I am a quadriplegic (with an injury of C7 to T2). I have had a disability for many years, I used to be controlling and not patient. I am now and must be not controlling and patient.

I can see my dad talking to God, saying, "She always has to learn everything the hard way." My dad would tell me, if I had nothing to worry about, I would find something to worry about. I felt I lost everything. I felt jipped and thought God had a different set of rules for me. We can feel desperate, alone, and feel nothing is ever going to change. If you look back on your life, you can see where God used His divine intervention at places; He is our help.

I knew this book was special when I was researching the Bible. I love the Psalms because they sound like a desperate plea for God to stop and look at us. Psalms 70:5 says, "But I am poor and needy; hasten o me O God! You are my help and deliverer; O Lord do not delay." Nobody ever talks about if God says, "No." I have never heard a sermon about it. The word from God could sometimes be no or not now. He wants us to feel good, and I wish I was healed on earth. He could just exhale, and it would be done.

It is not always a sin, a lesson, or a way through. Bad times happen to us all; we learn from our mistakes. We all learn to deal with a crisis differently, we must find a new normal. It is not easy to trust God when all seems hopeless.

It is a good read and at times funny. It is like I am right there, talking to you. This book has been helpful for me being in the Word of God and thinking about caregivers and having a disability. The Scriptures are in the book, right there for you. I would pray for God to direct my words. It took eight years to sit down and write a book, I knew it was the right time to do it and did. When I thought I was done with this book, I was not; I would be flooded with ideas for this book. Even at night, I would be woken up and be flooded with ideas. Just when I thought I was finished with the book, I got flooded again what to write.

As I typed the book, I knew I had something special in this book. I drop everything, and I get stuff caught in my motor wheelchair all the time. God always makes a good thing out of something so bad, like our disability. "For we are what he has made us, created in Christ Jesus for good works, which God prepared beforehand to be our way of life" (Ephesians 2:10).

Having a disability or being a caregiver to a disabled person is not a shock to God. He still has a purpose for us all, even with a disability or caring for one with a disability. This book addresses what is not talked about having a disability, like if God says the word *no* or *not now*. It also addresses when we ask for something, it must be in God's will.

This book is backed up with Scriptures. I feel it will help others, and I believe my book will not only help the disabled but the military. Those that are brave and are beefcakes go into the military, doing it all to leaving and needing help with the simplest of daily tasks like brushing your teeth and dressing. The military people being disabled is a shock to them. Life never goes as planned, being disabled is their life now. To me, being disabled is like having your body not obey you.

As I researched the scriptures of the Bible, I learned all God's promises are for the disabled and the caregivers too. I thought things could not get worse—they did. I had an addiction to prescribed medicine, lost my ability to move like I wanted to, went blind, and had a stroke. I am stuck with a disability and a speech impediment and must move forward because life still goes on. I was first a Christian, wife, mother, and a social worker. I took care of everything, and now, I was the one who needed help: catheters, diapers, and having sponge baths. This book is real and an honest way to deal with a disability and the caregivers that help us. Disability does not just happen to you; it happens to our caregivers and those who love us too. Crisis happens to us all; it may be a death of a loved one, an illness, or loss of job. We all have a crisis. Do we just take the good and leave the bad? Do we go on in life or hide out in our homes? God still has a plan for us, and we never walk alone, even when we feel like it.

CHAPTER 1

Wikipedia free encyclopedia says:

The Kübler-Ross model, or the five stages of grief, postulates a series of emotions experienced by terminally ill patients prior to death, wherein the five stages are denial, anger, bargaining, depression and acceptance.

The model was first introduced by Swiss psychiatrist Elisabeth Kübler-Ross in her 1969 book, *On Death and Dying*, and was inspired by her work with terminally ill patients. Motivated by the lack of curriculum in medical schools on the subject of death and dying, Kübler-Ross examined death and those faced with it at the University of Chicago medical school. Kübler-Ross' project evolved into a series of seminars which, along with patient interviews and previous research, became the foundation for her book. Since the publication of "On Death and Dying", the Kübler-Ross model has become accepted by the general public; however, its validity is not consistently supported by the majority of research.

Kübler-Ross noted later in life that the stages are not a linear and predictable progression and that she regretted writing them in a way that was misunderstood. Rather, these are a collation of five common experiences for the bereaved that can occur in any order, if at all.

Kübler-Ross says there are five phases of death: bargaining, denial, anger, depression, and acceptance. The stages of death were exactly the same for me in disability. My favorite phase is denial. None of the other phases worked for me. You see, I had Tim and two girls to think of, I thought times such as these (paralyzed), they were watching. I was not able to show anger or depression. Trust me, I felt them. I held together for them; they were my motivation. God got an earful because He can handle it. *If I panicked, they would too*, I thought.

When I was thirty-eight years old, I had pain in my arms and my MRI showed I had syringomyelia, a watery cyst in my spinal cord from fluid from the brain draining. I was not able to control things. When I dropped a can of tomatoes, I knew something was wrong.

Don't you hate MRIs? They are so loud and right in your face and you must lie completely still. Sure, I will be completely still! I used to do everything, drive, hold a job, and I liked to cook and clean. I was a mom to a seven-year-old and a ten-year-old. I was a Sicilian who liked to take care of my family.

I had a decompression surgery where they put a shunt in my head so it could drain brain fluid properly and I would feel much better. I believed I would have minimal damage to some nerves and go back to life as normal.

It was Christmastime, December 2008. I thought I had already been through the worst. This year, I called the year of hardness. My dad, grandma and, soon after, godmother died. I lost my ability to work, walk, home, and routine. I thought, *How is this happening?* How? I am a child God, right! "For all who are led by the Spirit of God are children of God" (Romans 8:14). Where I had the procedure done, I was left for a long time in the hall being under construction. I was hurt and shaking. I felt like I was in a nightmare I couldn't wake up from or control. I kept asking workers of the hospital for help but they ignored me. I thought, *How dare they?*

My husband and boss saw my medication was very late and I was left in the hall. I even heard others at the nursing station being so inappropriate. They called a patient activist, and I was moved to a VIP floor where they would take care of rich athletes. I was experiencing pain in my neck. I had a good friend stay a night with me.

I was so worried about Tim and the girls, I changed hospitals close to home. I was not able to sit up. It was my physical therapy goal. Coffee and food were not appealing to me. I usually love those things. I remember missing holidays and my husband and girls. I held the girls every morning. I was forced to be okay. I knew the girls and my husband, Tim, were watching me. I felt like the staff and doctors were watching too. How was I going to act at times such as these?

So I figured, God knows what my thoughts on my mind are. My thoughts were hopeless, and I complained in my head. I do not think God wants me to think this way. I thought others who complain and have their illness as their identity were weak or attention-seeking. Imagine my surprise when I found out all my thoughts were wrong. I now have to practice my thoughts. I had the part about not complaining down but not my thoughts. Oh my gosh, I had no idea. Let me make it clear. *For me*, it was the same. I did not say complaining about your disability was wrong, *for me* it was.

I miss my kids being little. I get when others say, "You will blink your eyes and your children will be grown." Boy, is that so true! I now look back on the kids being small and before I had a disability. I am all done with that life, kids are older so a new chapter. God will work with my disability to help others.

To be haughty and boastful can be attention-seeking behavior that says "Look at me, look at me. Look what I have been through!" It is important to not make yourself better than others or an idol more important than God. I would think, all the time, I was better than others.

I read when the Israelites made a gold calf their god and thought that they were dumb. They saw the Red Sea parted, had a cloud of fire to follow. I would think, *How stupid can you be?* I bet in God's world, there is no room for that stuff. It is a fine line, being haughty and boastful and idol worship. Even yourself, having a disability and making others feel bad for you and you could easily suck it up and run with it. It can be easy to do. Try our hardest to not be haughty and boastful. We can have hardness in this life on earth, God can see our whole lives. I take comfort in this.

The biblical Scripture is for us. It is easy not to see that. What is easy is to focus on all the bad. I believe if you publicly seek self-pity, it can be idolatry. Remember, I likened it to, "Look at all the bad that has happened to me. I have suffered too much, see?" I said publicly. I think it is okay to tell God how you feel because the Lord can handle it. I am grateful because if you unscrewed my head, it will shock you, all I feel and think. I can feel, at times, Scriptures are for the righteous, and there so many times I do not feel righteous. See, we need the Lord's mercy or else we would be goners.

I must pray all the time, trust me. I am glad God does not see my disability as a hindrance to what He has planned. Others, and maybe you, think your disability means you have no future or God has no plan for you.

God works on a purpose for us at times. You must be ready in God's eyes to work. God chose us. We can feel forsaken by God with our disability. We are in good company. Even Jesus was forsaken on the cross. He was mocked and in great pain on the cross. He showed the ultimate self-control ever. Crucifixion had to hurt much.

Listen, we all handle crisis differently; it takes a while to find a new normal. We used to have our church, family, and friends in Michigan. Here in Kentucky, we had to fully depend on God. I used to talk a lot and was not alone if I did not want to be alone. There was always someone to call to come over and stay with me. This was before the stroke, and I had a friend I cooked with. We liked to plan meals and dinners. She would bring an extra pot and something to carry dinner home. I went to being active to no longer being as active. See, with or without a disability, God will still work in our lives. It made me feel normal; I am so impatient and must work on it.

It has been years since I was paralyzed, and years from the stroke, and I still haven't reached acceptance. I love ignorant bliss; what I do not know cannot hurt me. Unfortunately I knew. In the denial phase, I would get hurt. I would try to do things before like work and cook. The truth was, I was not the same. I would be different for a long time. I would hurt myself, pass out from low blood pressure, burn myself, and I was in and out of the hospital. At the hospital, everyone would say I was so inspirational. I never felt that way. If you unscrewed my head and saw all I complained to God, about it would shock you.

I want to be healed so bad; I can see it, I can see me doing all I used to do. I miss driving, cooking, sleeping on my tummy, and cleaning. Oh, wearing heels too! I wonder if those who became disabled dream the same way as me? I dreamed like I am healed. I do not think there was a time that I dreamed with my disability. I see myself driving Hope and Grace to school and hiking Natural Bridge and walking the dog in the park. I see me making snacks for my family. I can see me doing all the shopping and cleaning. There is also a KitchenAid and some new pans that I want to use but my body will not let me. I will say my body will not obey me. You know what to do and have a brain inside you and your body will not listen.

I feel like they are torturing me. I want to garden and can too. I am a Sicilian woman who does not grow my own tomatoes! There must be a disability present to not be able to do that! I want to be healed so bad. I remember to not rely on my feelings because I cannot do much. I tell God all my feelings because He can handle that. I believe Romans 8:28, "We know that all things work out together for those who love God, who are called according to His purpose." *All*—not some—but *all things*. That includes disability. Yes, disability. I love the book of Romans, it's full of treasures. "What can we say about these things? If God is for us, who is against us" (Romans 8:31). Powerful, right? If I got healed on earth, I would need to be sedated. What I do now is what I can do—pray and do good.

Now with a disability, I was not able to laugh or wear pretty shoes! I have what is called drop foot on the right foot; my right leg and the foot would fall off my chair, I would not even know. I think my family are used to it, even my kids will walk by and put my foot up. For this reason, I do not get to wear heels. I missed out on the platform heels that matched your legs. I like to call them hooker heels. Would I wear them? You bet I would! Sometimes I would get my foot pinned under my chair and would never know. Tim worried about, the drop foot.

Let's talk about leg shaking and phantom pains; they are nothing you can control. Leg shaking is spasticity and phantom pains, Wikipedia defines like this:

> Phantom pain sensations are described as perceptions that an individual experience relating to a limb or an organ that is not physically part of the body. Limb loss is a result of either removal by amputation or congenital limb deficiency. However, phantom limb sensations can also occur following nerve avulsion or spinal cord injury. Sensations are recorded most frequently following the amputation of an arm or a leg but may also occur following the removal of a breast or an internal organ. Phantom limb pain is the feeling of pain in an absent limb or a portion of a limb. The pain sensation varies from individual to individual." Spasticity is a defined, by the Christopher Reeve Foundation, are "side effect of paralysis that varies from mild muscle stiffness to severe, uncontrollable leg movements. Generally, doctors now call conditions of extreme muscle tension spastic hypertonia (SH). It may occur in association with spinal cord injury, multiple sclerosis, cerebral palsy, or brain trauma.

Now I have trouble and experience of the phantom pains. The family and I would laugh when the pains would happen; it was funny to us. The phantom pains are the worst to deal with. What helps is Tim showing me my feet. I do not understand, it just helps. Some phantom pains you are stuck with. Sometimes I feel like a block of ice is on my legs. It is not true, and I get freezing, my skin would be cold. Amazing what the mind can do. I could feel so cold and would need my blankets on me and we can feel the cold on my body. The worst reoccurring phantom pain would be *the wedgie*! I remember what that would feel like. I have the feeling of one and not have one and would not. The mind is powerful.

I was with Grace, my oldest girl, and her husband, Andrew. We were talking and I had a bottle of water. I said, "I must have dropped my cap." I had the cap on my drink the whole time. That is exactly what I get confused with a stroke. I also could blame it on old age. Stroke, yeah, yeah, I will milk this as long as I can!

In the denial phase, I would get hurt and would never know it until Tim would show me my bruised foot and a swollen foot. I used to be able to run in heels. The girls (my kids) always think about *Jurassic World*, they would wonder why the lead actress in it could run in heels. They would think, *Mom could run in heels if she was mobile*. Things are superficial like heels but important to me.

I was in the hospital all the time with an infection. I got numerous blood injections and I would not want to see the needle or the blood. I was honest and would not look and have the staff at the hospital cover the blood with a towel. I was a chicken. I even got so many potassium shots. They hurt, and I begged them to inject me where I did not feel.

One time, I was in the hospital and was septic. I had bedsores on my feet from not being properly elevated. They gave me an MRI on the feet. I am sure if you are paralyzed, you know all about bedsores. They take a long recovery. The MRI showed the bedsores entered my bones, I would never know and had no pain. The MRI showed I broke my Achilles heel; I never knew how I did it and was glad I could not feel it. I am used to my feet being bruised and swollen, I never paid much attention to it—I am sure I banged into something. I would be septic and would be out of my mind, and I remembered I wanted to be left alone; and since I was unable to move, I kept on pulling the covers over my head. If they cannot see me, then they will go away, right?

Laughing, I loved. There is a show I love called *Impractical Jokers*. This show is so fun, I would take a blood pressure pill before I watched or I could pass out. I learned the hard way; I saw *Scary Movie* where they spoofed *Signs*, the movie, and laughed so hard in my head, I passed out in front of my family. Now I make a noise and say, "That is so funny!" I watch *Impractical Jokers* and forget any problems I have. I love when my youngest, Hope, is in my hospital bed and snuggles me and we watch it together. Outside I must act like I am cool about it, but I was so excited on the inside because I get to hold her and watch with her. I had to act calm about her snuggling with me. I used to always snuggle my kids, before I was injured, on the couch.

When I became paralyzed, my youngest, Hope, was a little girl. My kids needed me. My kids saw me working, driving, cooking, and cleaning the house and snuggled them to me needing so much help. Things I used to hide from Tim and others are all exposed, like Tim helping me shave my legs, bathing, dyeing my hair, and even using the bathroom. How vulnerable can I get! One time, I even got off the oven door and hooked it on my chair. Who does that? Apparently me. I even ran over my sweet daughter's leg two times and went to the emergency room. The same day, she was treated by the same doctor at the hospital who remembered us. I was so embarrassed and told the truth. We were trying to clean out the fridge, I used to clean it each week before I went shopping. I tried to do things like I did before and I, or someone else, got hurt. I remember a time my in-laws were over and I rammed my chair into the stereo, and I shattered the glass cover on it. It was a big mess. I tried to act like it was not a big deal, but inside, I was so embarrassed.

My circumstances got bad to worse; there is no way to get here without God being with me, I should not survive or exist. I have been septic four times and lived. I would ask God how many times can a girl get? He knows the answer. We do not walk alone, bad things happen to good people all the time. I just happen to be that kind of person that had the bad happen to them. Are we supposed to take the good in our lives and not the bad?

> But while everybody was asleep, an enemy came
> and sowed the weeds among the wheat and then
> went away. (Matthew 13:5)

> Let both grow together until the harvest; and at
> harvest time I will tell the reapers, collect the weeds
> first and bind them in bundles to be burned, but
> the wheat into my barn. (Matthew 13:30)

I think the devil tried so many times to have me dead. I remember a time that stands out, I was in the eleventh grade and went on a canoe trip with a youth group on the Rife River in Michigan. I have never been canoeing before and had a partner assumed too this was not a problem. We had an accident. A bad one that the youth group would not know. My youth group went ahead of us. The river looked so calm on the top. We tipped over at a tree that had very small rapids. I looked for the air pocket under the canoe but there was not one, I had to kick out under it. I opened my eyes and saw brown and green; the water was murky, and I could not see a thing. I remembered, at this time, my dad and I at the St. Claire Shores, Michigan, pool and how long I could hold my breath. Dad would count and I would go under and hold my breath.

Just when I thought I could not hold my breath any longer, I was grabbed out of the water by a stranger. Thank God! I remember being pulled to the bank, and it was not shallow there. My fingers tried to hold on the edge, and my body was being dragged to the bank of the river. It looked like calm water on top. I guess there was a strong current. My friend was still under the water and was pulled out. I saw her spit up water and cry. We were saved by a group of people that felt sure they needed to take a break. They were in the right place at the right time and kept on saying they did not know why they needed to stop, they had only been canoeing for three hours. Thank God! Our canoe was stuck under a tree, unusable, and they took us on theirs. I learned to canoe that day from them. God made a good situation out of something bad. Each bump made my poor partner cry and be afraid. We were three and a half hours late. When we got home, I was called by the youth pastor who felt bad.

I went to the town fireworks and saw them land the helicopter and put it away. I wanted to fade in the background, not be noticed; in my chair, that is not possible and I get looks. People are so curious and afraid of me. I got to be first where I wanted sit at the fireworks by the fire department. Tim even got a chair, they were being so nice to us. I do not expect to get any special treatment, but I do get special treatment. I used to like attention, and now, I feel I get too much. I graciously accept it because it helps those around you to know you are comfortable.

I am in a season to wait now and must live in the moment. I live one day at a time and practice living in the moment. I was watching the fireworks and thinking that I could have missed out seeing them. If you have a disability and want to stay in your house, don't, because you will be missing out. People are curious and stare, and others may talk to you; it goes with a disability. Do not miss out in your life, it is so easy to turn into yourself and make your disability an excuse, life goes on and you decide if it goes on with you or without you. We all can handle our disability differently; you may have to start over and be a part of life. You may be disabled and it is bad for you, but there are good times to be had with or without a disability.

I do not want to make my disability my identity. I really do not want to deal with it. However, I must and refuse to let it have any power over me. It is too easy to let it be the only thing about you. My kids are watching, and I want to display how to act at hard times. Only with God's help can I do this. There is nothing special about me, I do not have it all figured out. You may have a disability but life still happens and goes on with or without you. Your disability is a crisis for you and not others.

My life is different now. When my kids were little and if they had a temperature, I would sleep on the couch with the kids on me. I was never able to relax when my kids were sick, like a lot like some of you. There was a time when I was mobile, we were making iced tea and it was put in a glass container and it broke and Hope (my youngest) was burnt and slipped on it. I saw she was hurt and I scooped her up in my arms and put her in the cold shower. My baby was hurt and I sprang into action, we mothers do that. I think we are programmed to jump into action with our kids. With a disability, I do not get jump to action right away, I was paralyzed and had a stroke. I look at pictures from before the disability and with a disability and see a difference with how my family looks. My family and I were devastated of having a disability. Tim talked to me about what the family was having to deal with disability. He said it felt like it was us against the world. We had to go on with life.

What I learned when I had the stroke was to not compare myself to anyone educationally, physically, and financially. These were things I used to strive for. The world would see these things as being good and to strive for them. I do not think these things are bad; I just see it differently now. It is okay now to not be the smartest, prettiest, or richest person; I felt free. Comparison can be a trap. I should know, I used to compare everything. It took a disability for me to learn! I saw on the television that supermodels have low self-esteem. they would get told what is wrong and get compared to everyone. I watch a lot of television and see commercials for burger places—so deceitful. They will have a beautiful model taking a big seductive bite of a burger. First if you eat a ton of burgers, you will never look like that. Second I do not know one person that looks like that.

So I have a funny story that is, unfortunately, true. I was in college and the show *90210* was popular, and I thought I would fill in my eyebrows like the girl actors on the show—big mistake. I filled them in too much and walked around with these filled eyebrows that were obvious and bad.

Comparison is tiring and not being content. We must be content with ourselves, even with a disability. Even being a caretaker, you must be content with all you have.

I listen to God and I think He must know it. The truth is, God used to talk to me when I used to use the bathroom or in my sleep when I was the quietest. It is not like I hear an audible voice. Funny, I think, I have had so much on my mind when I did all things like work. God talks to me in reading, music, or a flood of ideas.

He has a purpose for me, even with a disability. He is not done with me with or without a disability. Anyone who would talk to me or see me would not think so. I can sometimes see on their face and from their nonverbals. "Poor Anna, glad it is not me." I used to think the same thing. I have a speech impediment, and I am paralyzed. My injury is C7 and T2. He still has a plan for me now, like this—disabled. Who are you around the most? Caregivers. Be the best person you can be with a disability, you can minister to them. At one point, I was in the hospital so much, I thought I had a ministry to whoever came in my room. I had to be happy but I was not; I was out of my mind, no makeup, and at my worst. I did not feel like ministering. I was more chicken of what God would think. I always thought of that so I acted fine. I will write it again, God has a plan for all of us with or without a disability. I love the scripture in Jeremiah 29:10–14:

> For thus say the Lord: Only when Babylon's seventy years are completed will I visit you, and I will fulfill to you my promise and bring you back to this place. For I surely know the plans I have for you, says the Lord, plans for your welfare, and not for harm, to give you a future with hope. Then when you call upon me and come and pray to me, I will hear you. When you search for me, you will find me; if you seek me with all your heart, I will let you find me, says the Lord, and I will restore your fortunes and gather you from all the nations and all the places where I have driven you says the Lord and I will bring you back to the place from which I sent you into exile. Is not God the same He was yesterday and before.

> For nothing will be impossible with God. (Luke 1:37).

> Now faith is the assurance of things hoped for, the conviction of things not seen. Indeed, by faith ancestors received approval. By faith we understand that the worlds were prepared by the word of God, so that what is seen was made from things that are not visible. (Hebrews 11:1–3)

> Now faith is the assurance of things hoped for,
> the conviction of things not seen. Indeed, by
> faith our ancestors received approval. By faith we
> understand that the worlds were prepared by the
> word of God, so that what is seen was made from
> things that are not visible. (Romans 8:28)

That gives me hope, the Lord may use us for some good. Scripture is relevant for us *today*. We could think of it is letters, a history for us to enjoy. Having a disability, we are called even more to let our God and the way we live as an *anchor* of our soul.

> So that through two unchangeable things, in
> which it is impossible that God would prove
> false, we who have taken refuge might be strongly
> encouraged to seize the hope set before us. We
> have this hope, a sure and steadfast anchor of the
> soul, a hope that enters the inner shrine behind
> the curtain, where Jesus, a forerunner on our
> behalf, has entered, having become a high priest
> forever according to the order of Melchizedek.
> (Hebrews 6:18–20)

CHAPTER 2

We have to please God with a disability or not. We do not get a get-out-of-jail card because our bodies would not work. I often say that my body will not obey me. I am afraid of fire, and to me, there is no such thing as control. I used to be controlling. If you are disabled, you do not get to have any control. All things change. You know what is so hard? What I sill struggle with? Privacy. If you have a disability, you do not have the luxury to have any privacy that you used to have before your injury. I would never have anyone dress me, bathe me, and change me. Come on, I cannot be the only one. This is how I deal with it. A day at a time. I have been embarrassed so many times but survived. I think this will be no different. I know you must hate your disability and what goes with it. I was changed by a guy. I could see he was uncomfortable and I did what I usually do. I was thirty-eight years old and told him, in a funny way, "We (women) do not usually look like this." We both felt embarrassed.

This is smart. Have you ever heard of the Socrates filter test?

> In ancient Greece, Socrates (the famous philosopher) was visited by an acquaintance of his. Eager to share some juicy gossip, the man asked if Socrates would like to know the story he'd just heard about a friend of theirs. Socrates replied that before the man spoke, he needed to pass the "Triple-Filter" test.
>
> The first filter, he explained, is *truth*. "Have you made absolutely sure that what you are about to say is true?" The man shook his head. "No, I actually just heard about it, and Socrates cut him

off. "You don't know for certain that it is true, then. Is what you want to say something good or kind?" Again, the man shook his head. "No! Actually, just the opposite. You see..." Socrates lifted his hand to stop the man speaking. "So you are not certain that what you want to say is true, and it isn't good or kind. One filter still remains, though, so you may yet still tell me. That is usefulness or necessity. Is this information useful or necessary to me?"

A little defeated, the man replied, "No, not really." "Well, then," Socrates said, turning on his heel. "If what you want to say is neither true, nor good or kind, nor useful or necessary, please don't say anything at all."

Consider this. Before you answer a question or voice your opinion, ask yourself:

- Is it true?
- Is it good?
- Is it kind?
- Is it useful?
- Is it necessary?

If it passes these filters, speak up. If not, either find a tactful way to make a pass, or better still, keep it to yourself. Most people leave it at that and assume that the story is just about the information we spread.

What if the real truth behind it, however, is about the information we seek and create? Imagine how different the world would be if we only chose to seek or create information that was true, good, or useful. Imagine how different the world would be if we only chose to seek Socrates's information that was true, good, or useful?"

Makes you really think. There was a time I enjoyed gossip. To not be involved in gossips was hard, so I excuse myself to use the bathroom. I do not know what the people I worked with thought, I was always go to the bathroom. I was desperate and just knew gossip was wrong. I was the person who wanted to know all.

When I was first paralyzed, I was a lot like Scarlet from *Gone with the Wind*. Tomorrow is another day, right? It is how I survived. Now I was living to survive, not to live. I was at the hospital near home, and on Christmas Eve, Tim and the girls had Chinese dinner with my mom, not my Sicilian food I took much pride in. There was a girl on a motor wheelchair giving out candy canes and notes, saying Jesus loves you. She dressed up as an elf. I was so freaked out and told Tim my medicine was too much and I was seeing things like elves that told me God loves me. We are God's representatives, His ambassadors, God's ambassadors, no matter what is happening to us. How we are and act with a disability matters, and I am like so many others and do not always feel like I am fine. I feel others are watching, and I have a big responsibility to act a certain way. I do not want to be responsible for someone else's spiritualness. You know we could be.

Last night, my daughter Hope had a senior orientation at her school. We went and were in the back because there were no seats and the handicapped seat were full of others who really had no need of them. When you are disabled, the handicapped seat and parking are taken often to those who do not need them. Do you say anything? I do not and do not want to make them feel guilty or bad. It happens, and you have to learn how to deal with it. I do not expect any special treatment for my disability, it's just not my style. I would rather be a fly on the wall and not be seen; I want to hide and this wheelchair is not inconspicuous. At the meeting, it was packed full of students and their parents. The principal was talking about extra stuff, and while the principle was talking, many others got up, even the parents. I imagined if I was her and what I would say, "Sit your butts back down in your seats.

Others will not know all, but your caregivers would. The things we want to keep private are no longer hidden. Then how are we supposed to act with a disability? Just because we have disability does not mean we can turn into ourselves and not care how we look and act to others. I say practice, we all must practice this until we go to heaven. I must practice the fruits of the Spirit. Do I have all of them? No way, I try.

> His divine power has given us everything needed for life and Godliness., through the knowledge of Him who called by His own glory and goodness. Thus, He has given us, through these things, His precious and very great promises, so that them you may escape from the corruption that is in the world, because of lust, and may become participants of the divine nature. (2 Peter 1:3–11)

To me, if others are suffering and it does not affect me directly, it is different than if I am suffering. If I am directly affected and I suffer, it is a terrible thing. We act differently if we are suffering and someone else is suffering. I believe we are to think of others and pray for others. Whatever you do, think of others. Listen, the people will go on, the world will go on with or without you, disabilities and all. It is so important to get yourself off your mind and think of others, not all you have endured and suffered. Think, if you turn too much into yourself, you can forget. With a disability, you can focus on yourself and your identity can be just your disability. I do not want my disability to be who I am. I am a Christian, wife, mother, and a social worker who happened to get paralyzed and had a stroke. It sounds bad, I know. If you have a disability, you suffer some and we must persevere. Perseverance is hard, and I wish I did not have to deal with disability. I feel like I have no other choice to learn this; disability makes me deal with this. Darn!

According to the *Free Dictionary* online, *perseverance* is defined:

- imply determined continuance in a state or in a course of action.
- <u>Perseverance</u> suggests effort maintain in spite of difficulties or long continued application; it is used in a favorable sense: *The scientist's perseverance finally paid off in a coveted prize.*

- *Persistence*, which may be used in a favorable or unfavorable sense, implies steadfast, unremitting continuance in spite of opposition or protest: an annoying persistence a belief.
- *Tenacity* is a dogged and determined holding on: the stubborn tenacity of a salesman. Also, steady persistence in adhering to a course of action, a belief, or a purpose; steadfastness.

I look to see what the Bible says about persistence.

> Seek the Lord and his strength, seek his presence continually. I recommend you read the whole passage. (1 Chronicles 16:11)

> Trust in the Lord with all your heart, and do not rely on your own insight. In all your ways acknowledge him, and he will make straight your paths. (Proverbs 3:5–6)

Again another one to read the passage.

> But the one who endures to the end will be saved. (Matthew 24:13)

> And not only that, but we also boast in our sufferings, knowing that suffering produces endurance, and endurance produces character, and character produces hope, and hope does not disappoint us, because God's love has been poured into our hearts through the Holy Spirit that has been given to us. (Romans 5:3–5)

Great! I have endurance, character, and hope. I have much like you have much to boast about. "So let us not grow weary in doing what is right, for we will reap at harvest time, if we do not give up. So then, whenever we have an opportunity, let us work for the good of all, and especially for those of the family of faith" (Galatians 9:9–10). This scripture proves to me that it is not about us. It talks about other Christians, family. Just because we have a disability, it does not mean we get to never think of others. It is so easy to say, "Poor me." Fight against this. Think about how you can help others intentionally. It will help others and get your mind off you.

I hate riding in elevators now! I do not mind if it is just Tim and me. I hate to be paralyzed and must look at strangers' butts. Come on, you know what it means if you're in a wheelchair; not flattering at all—butts. Let me tell you, if you're paralyzed, you must deal with this too. Tim and I went for an appointment at a hospital and I had to let down my car ramp to my handicap van, I acted all cool and could feel people looking at me. It is not every day you see that. My purse was blocking my view, I drove my chair wrong off the ramp, and I was sure to fall. Great, did I mention it was valet parking? I wanted to fade in the background and ended up making a spectacle of myself. I was told by the bystanders they were afraid and scared I would fall also—so much for being cool and fading in the background. Do you know if you are in a wheelchair and see others in a wheelchair, there is a secret nod of the head we give each other? This true and it is intently done; just in a nod, we understand what the other has to deal with and to say we know what it is like to have a disability.

Remember the prayer the Our Father? "Our Father in heaven, hallowed be your name, your kingdom come, Your *will be done*, on earth as it is in heaven. Give us this day our daily bread. And forgive us are debts, as we also forgiven our debtors. And do not bring us to the time of temptation but rescue us for the evil one." For you forgive other trespasses, your heavenly Father will also forgive you; but if you do not forgive others, neither will your Father forgive your trespasses.

Did you get the part where He says *give us this day*? I live one day at a time because I believe I am called to do that. From the time I get my head off the pillow to laying my head back down on the pillow, I seek God before every day I get up and I have to make a choice everyday how I plan on doing. Not to fall in self-pity or into myself. I think the Our Father prayer is like a guide on how to pray. I say the prayer and then break it up and pray it specific to me. Thank God, His mercies are new every morning. "The steadfast love of the Lord never ceases, His mercies never come to an end; they are new every morning; great is they faithfulness. 'The Lord is my portion,' says my soul, 'therefore I will hope in Him'" (Lamentations 3:22–24).

We have right now, and at times such as these, the Lord gives us confidence. Look at the following scriptures:

> And I am sure of this, that he who began a good work in you will bring it to completion at the day of Jesus Christ. (Philippians 1:6)

> Let us then with confidence draw near to the throne of grace, that we may receive mercy and find grace to help in time of need. (Hebrews 4:16)

> "So we can confidently say 'The Lord is my helper; I will not fear; what can man do to me?'" (Hebrews 13:6)

Even with a disability, we can have confidence right now.

It is normal and okay if you are not handling your disability well. I am always having a hard time with it all and all that goes with it, and I have been disabled for many years. There is a lot; caregivers and those with a disability who knows all the things that go with a disability. Tell me where in the Bible it is where it says this mortal life is carefree. I used to think that way. A new normal we had to find. Our problems just do not go away. That would be so nice. I think we are and should live one day at a time.

I now do not like fires or water. If you have a disability, you will know what I mean. We had a kitchen fire once and I was in my room and had not had the stroke and had my normal voice. Hope was making popcorn over the stove and went to the bathroom and forgot about it. She went back to the stove and flames were everywhere. She ran back and yelled fire! Grace and I thought she said spider in a southern Accent. Grace was with me in the room and jumped on

Tim's bed, in one leap, and screamed. Hope said again, "Fire! Not spider!" So I had Hope leash the dog and get out and flag down the fire truck. I told Grace I was I was going to call 9-1-1 and tell them where I was and get out. She did not want to leave me. I yelled to her to get out. I am sure I scared her by the way I yelled. I meant business. There I was, stuck in bed, worried if they all got out.

You know, I did not think of fire or being hurt. As a mom, you just put your kids first. Tim came right home and we had a family meeting and ice cream for dinner. Grace cried during the meeting. In her eyes, Mom is supposed to take care of everything and make it all okay. I told them all I was sorry we had to go through this. It was good for Grace to cry and be angry. She loved me so much, she had the not-me-disabled or the active me, this was not fixable. It was the first time she dealt with all that happened, not easy for her. We talked, we talked honestly. Hope was just there and listened. I wanted to scoop them up and tell them all would be fine. So I told them to look; we survived this and will survive more tough times to come.

One time, Hope was sick and had to stay at the hospital, so I wanted to stay the night with her. She was in pain and her dad and I wanted to fix it. If your kid is messed with, you get angry. You do what you can only do, pray. I said to Tim, in the hall at the hospital, "I dare you to make me leave and move this chair!"

He said he could not take care of me and Hope. The way he said it was serious, I knew by the way he said it I had to leave. When you have a disability, you really cannot do the things you want, like I wanted to stay with Hope, stay at the hospital. He was worried. In his mind, who would drain me, give me medicine, and my blood dropping with all that was going on with Hope. He was worried about everyone. He stayed after he got me settled. I felt gibed again. I was the mom. The one who would always stay. When you have a disability, you feel gibed; your role changes.

Having a disability, we get sick more often, recovery takes longer. I used to stay up till 11:00 p.m., now start to get sleepy at 8:00 p.m. I do not get sick often, but having a disability, I get sick bad; it goes with the territory. I got pneumonia and so did my caregiver,

Tim. I knew what it was and made him see a doctor. What is with guys and going to see a doctor? I felt it and knew it and acted quickly, you have to. There is a trick to it, really. I learned, for this was my sixth time having it, to sit up as you sleep. It went away and all was good. There was one time, I got pneumonia in the hospital and a code was called and people, including the doctor, tried to put a tube down my nose. I was not having that! They felt panicky, but I hold myself together in times of panic; I kept calm and breathed for them fine. They said I was aspirating and had trouble breathing. I felt I could breathe and they felt they were doing their best to help me.

Lucky me, I got a kidney infection which landed me in the hospital. I was shaking and felt cold, and Tim felt I was hot. He then took my temperature, it was 104.5 degrees. I would not know it was high, I felt cold. I have had sepsis four times and do not play with that. I went to the hospital, and they gave me some antibiotics and it worked to get the temperature down. No blankets for me, even though I felt cold and wanted them. My catheter was changed. I thought, *Welcome to my privates*. Great! See what a good example of privately invaded. I said I would rather be home than admitted. If you are paralyzed, they turn you every two hours. When I am sick, I want to sleep and not be touched. I was able to go home and be left alone. My eldest girl came over to watch me as Tim had to work. I slept for two days straight as my temperature was checked. Recovery surprised me; I was weak, and recovery took a while. I have had many infections and this one kicked my butt. I never expected to have a longer recovery.

Last weekend, Tim and I got to go to a band completion, and we got to see Hope lead the flutes. It was fun to see all the bands. There was one other boy in a wheelchair; he even had a tracheotomy. This is another reminder that things can always be worse. You may feel, with your disability, it can't be any worse—it can, it is. I see it sometimes when I feel self-pity. I think it can be worse; I think this keeps me going on in this life.

I felt self-pity in the sixth grade and never told anyone about an incident I had. I was in the sixth grade, and a petition was passed around to everyone in class and it said, "If you hate Anna, sign this."

The only people who refused to sign were my cousin and best friend. It was made because my sister's friends waited for me outside, one day. The day was sixth-grade kick day. These kinds of days went on and kick days scared me. So back to the petition. I had to ride the bus with some that signed. I wanted to cry but did not because I wanted them to see, they could not break me. I should have earned an acting award because my heart went in my stomach. I knew if I told my parents, they would feel bad for me and would do something about it; so I just knew it would end eventually and returning to school was hard, and I pretended it never happened. My parents were mad when I had a friend's dad call me a "dego" and told me I could never go to her house and she was not to be my friend.

We think good, read our Bible, go to Mass. We can think, we do not deserve this and another person who seems bad does not have a disability. We think, why us? Like I have to fight this, and I would think of celebrities who do not even believe in God and others who have it easy on earth. We do not deserve this. The answer I get in thought is, it is not any of our business. We should never think we are better than others. I think I am so much better than those others on *Dr. Phil*, *Cops*, or *Hoarders*. This is a dangerous thing to believe, a dangerous slippery slope. I must practice this. We are to be humbled; it is all over the Bible. Because it is in the Bible so much, it must be important.

I think God should answer prayers how we want; He answers prayers differently. Do you ever notice that? I think, I want God to make all the hard things go away. Sometimes my prayers sound like, "Give me, give me." I use God as a giver. He walks through the hard times with us. He cares so much about us, and I cannot be without Him. What I get from this is to keep asking God. I ask that He helps me get through the day. We must pray and go through the day with God. I just cannot imagine not praying, I see it as a necessity. I really believe living for yourself and your needs is dangerous. We live in the world that is so focused on me, my wants and needs.

God really knows our true intentions. We may think our true deep intentions are good. I love the prayer I pray daily.

Almighty and most merciful Father,
We have erred and strayed from thy ways like lost sheep,
We have followed too much the devices and desires of our own hearts,
We have offended against thy holy laws,
We have left undone those things which we ought to have done,
And we have done those things which we ought not to have done.
But thou, O Lord, have mercy upon us,
Spare thou those who confess their faults,
Restore thou those who are penitent,
According to thy promises declared unto mankind
In Christ Jesus our Lord;
And grant, O most merciful Father, for his sake,
That we may hereafter live a godly, righteous, and sober life,
To the glory of thy holy name.

I feel this covers the bases. I really believe apart from God, I can do nothing. I must live daily with him.

We can forget God's mighty power. It is not our place to ask Him why. It is not easy, but we should trust God. We have to trust when the bottom drops out; it could. Our disability feels like the bottom dropped out. It is exactly at those hard times we are never alone. It is hard to do when everything around you is falling apart. At times like these, our feelings can be negative.

Remember, His ways are not our ways. Look at Zechariah and St. Paul, Luke 1:5–25:

> In the days of King Herod of Judea, there was a priest named Zechariah, who belonged to the priestly order of Abijah. His wife was a descendant of Aaron, and her name was Elizabeth. Both of them were righteous before God, living blamelessly according to all the commandments and regulations of the Lord. But they had no

children, because Elizabeth was barren, and both were getting on in years. (Luke 1:5–7)

The scripture said, "Righteous before God." It is possible to be righteous before God. In the Old Testament, it said others did right or wrong in God's sight. For example, 2 Chronicles 24:2, Josiah did what was right in the sight of the Lord. all the days of the priest Jehosida.

Once when he was serving as priest before God and his section was on duty, he was chosen by lot, according to the custom of the priesthood, to enter the sanctuary of the Lord and offer incense. Now at the time of the incense offering, the whole assembly of the people was praying outside. Then there appeared to him an angel of the Lord, standing at the right side of the altar of incense. When Zechariah saw him, he was terri-fied; and fear overwhelmed him. But the angel said to him, "Do not be afraid, Zechariah, for your prayer has been heard. Your wife Elizabeth will bear you a son, and you will name him John. You will have joy and gladness, and many will rejoice at his birth, for he will be great in the sight of the Lord. He must never drink wine or strong drink; even before his birth he will be filled with the Holy Spirit. He will turn many of the people of Israel to the Lord their God. With the spirit and power of Elijah he will go before him, to turn the hearts of parents to their children, and the dis-obedient to the wisdom of the righteous, to make ready a people prepared for the Lord." Zechariah said to the angel, I know that this is so? For I am an old man, and my wife is getting on in years." The angel replied, "I am Gabriel. I stand in the presence of God, and I have been sent to speak to you and to bring you this good news. But now, because you did not believe my words, which will be fulfilled in their time, you will become mute, unable to speak, until the day these things occur" (note to self, believe angels). Meanwhile, the people were waiting for Zechariah, and wondered at his delay in the sanctuary. When he did come out, he could not speak to them, and they realized that he had seen a vision in the sanctuary. He kept motioning to them and remained unable to speak. When his time of service was ended, he went to his home.

After those days his wife Elizabeth conceived, and for five months she remained in seclusion. She said, "This is what the Lord has done for me when he looked favorably on me and took away the disgrace I have endured among my people." (Luke 1:8–25)

God can use anyone, even the disabled. He used Paul who was persecuting Christians.

Meanwhile Saul, still breathing threats and murder against the disciples of the Lord, went to the high priest and asked him for letters to the synagogues at Damascus, so that if he found any who belonged to the Way, men or women, he might bring them bound to Jerusalem. Now as he was going along and approaching Damascus, suddenly a light from heaven flashed around him. He fell to the ground and heard a voice saying to him, "Saul, Saul, why do you persecute me?" He asked, "Who are you, Lord?" The reply came, "I am Jesus, whom you are persecuting. But get up and enter the city, and you will be told what you are to do." The men who were traveling with him stood speechless because they heard the voice but saw no one. Saul got up from the ground, and though his eyes were open, he could see nothing; so, they led him by the hand and brought him into Damascus. For three days he was without sight, and neither ate nor drank.

Now there was a disciple in Damascus named Ananias. The Lord said to him in a vision, "Ananias." He answered, "Here I am, Lord." The Lord said to him, "Get up and go to the street called Straight, and at the house of Judas look for a man of Tarsus named Saul. At this moment he is praying, and he has seen in a vision a man named Ananias come in and lay his hands on him so that he might regain his sight." But Ananias answered, "Lord, I have heard from many about this man, how much evil he has done to your saints in Jerusalem; and here he has authority from the chief priests to bind all who invoke your name." But the Lord said to him, "Go, for he is an instrument whom I have chosen to bring my name before Gentiles and kings and before the people of Israel; I myself will show him how much he must suffer for the sake of my name." So Ananias went and entered the house. He laid his hands-on Saul and said, "Brother Saul, the Lord Jesus, who appeared to you on your way here, has sent me so that you may regain your sight and be filled with the Holy Spirit." And immediately something like scales fell from his eyes, and his sight was restored. Then he got up and was baptized, and after taking some food, he regained his strength. (Acts 9:1–19)

I think in these cases, God made something good come out of bad. What if your disability is for a reason you do not understand? What if your disability brings others salvation? It could!

One time I had to be transferred from the hospital in town to a hospital to Lexington, about two hours away. In the back with me, a woman was wondering how I survive and live. I told her that I pray all the time. She told me she never prayed before and wondered how to pray. I knew God must have put us together so I could help her learn how to talk to God.

Driving a motor wheelchair is not an easy thing. It is scary at first and hard to drive. I got a loaner motor wheelchair at the nursing home in which I lived. I relied on it for movement. There was a guy who had new knee replacements and had stiches up his two legs. Well, I was learning about the motor wheelchair and bumped into him more than once. His name was Kevin, and he we just thirty-seven years old. One time at the nursing home, I was going down to occupational therapy and it was him and me in an elevator. He saw me coming and covered his legs dramatically; he had a laugh. He did this each time we saw each other.

Did you know the motorized wheelchair goes three miles per hour? I asked how fast it can go and is how I found out. I tested this one time at a strip mall but did not tell anyone. I zoomed by the windows of different stores, what they must have thought. Poor Tim did not know until it was too late. One time, when I was still learning the chair, I went out to lunch with others from my church. I tried to be so cool and ran into a table and tilted it. Thank God my deacon was there and caught it. It was topped with water and coffee glasses and made a loud noise. All those around the table gasped, and I was embarrassed. I acted cool, like I knocked down tables before.

After five years, I had a physical therapy appointment and they asked me what I wanted in a chair. I said I wanted to wear high heels. Everybody laughed, but I was serious—dead serious. They said they never heard it before. They meant color. I said, with my speech impediment, I like purple. I got a new chair. Oh lastly, I ran into a man at a Walmart lunch meat counter with it because this chair goes back and forth. We did not know how to respond. I said sorry while

I thought it was kind of funny. He took my lead and laughed. All I could think was thank God, it could have ended so bad I could have taken him out.

I think some of the old testament is boring me. I think God must like barbecue and smelly stuff like incense.

The Lord said to Moses: "Take sweet spices, stacte, and onycha, and galbanum, sweet spices with pure frankincense (an equal part of each), and make an incense blended as by the perfumer, seasoned with salt, pure and holy; and you shall beat some of it into powder, and put part of it before the covenant] in the tent of meeting where I shall meet with you; it shall be for you most holy. When you make incense according to this composition, you shall not make it for yourselves; it shall be regarded by you as holy to the Lord. Whoever makes any like it to use as perfume shall be cut off from the people." (Exodus 30:34–38)

I get when it is said, "What it means to be in the world but not part of it." John 17:16 says, "They do not belong to the world, as I do not belong to the world. They said to them, 'You are from below, I am from above; you are from this world, I am not of this world.'" Is not God the same He was yesterday and before? Hebrews 13:8 says Jesus Christ is the same yesterday and today and forever. If that is true, then Jeremiah is true. Did you read the whole book to see what context the Scripture is written? He said, "I sent you to exile." We still get the bad circumstances of sin.

But the scripture has imprisoned all things under the power of sin, so that what was promised through faith in Jesus Christ might be given to those who believe. We reap what we sow. (Galatians 3:22)

Do not be deceived; God is not mocked, for you reap whatever you sow. If you sow to your own flesh, you reap corruption from the flesh but if you sow to the Spirit, you will reap eternal life from the Spirit. So, let us not grow weary in doing what is right, for we will reap at harvest time, if we do not give up. So then, whenever we have an opportunity, let us work for the good of all, and especially for those of the family of faith. (Galatians 6:7–10)

We are never alone. We are ambassadors for God. We should be an example of all who we see, with and without a disability. In

Galatians, the fruit of the Spirit is love, joy, peace, patience, kindness, generosity, faithfulness, gentleness, and self-control. There is no law against such like such things. And those who belong to Christ Jesus have crucified the flesh with its passions and desires. If we live by the spirit, we must have God's help. Who can be like this totally? We must have divine intervention.

"As long as I am in the world, I am the light of the world" (John 5:9). Jesus was talking here and healing a blind guy. Read the whole thing.

> In the beginning was the Word, and the Word was with God, and the Word was God. He was in the beginning with God. All things came into being through him, and without him not one thing came into being. What has come into being in him was life, and the life was the light of all people. The light shines in the darkness, and the darkness did not overcome it. (John 1:1–5)

Your life should reflect light.

> "Now my soul is troubled. And what should I say—'Father, save me from this hour?' No, it is for this reason that I have come to this hour. Father, glorify your name." Then a voice came from heaven, "I have glorified it, and I will glorify it again." The crowd standing there heard it and said that it was thunder. Others said, "An angel has spoken to him." Jesus answered, "This voice has come for your sake, not for mine. Now is the judgment of this world; now the ruler of this world will be driven out. And I, when I am lifted up from the earth, will draw all people to myself." He said this to indicate the kind of death he was to die. The crowd answered him,

"We have heard from the law that the Messiah remains forever. How can you say that the Son of Man must be lifted up? Who is this Son of Man?" Jesus said to them, "The light is with you for a little longer. Walk while you have the light, so that the darkness may not overtake you. If you walk in the darkness, you do not know where you are going. While you have the light, believe in the light, so that you may become children of light." (John 12:20–36)

You know what stands out to me? Verse 20, where it says, "Now my soul is troubled." We can forget He was human and He said all this when His circumstances were not good and He talked about His death. I have begged so many times for God to not let me suffer any. It is nice to know He gets when our souls are troubled. I once had a dream; in all my dreams, I can feel, walk, and talk., I was on a rocky path with God. I told Him, "Please change your mind, I am not handling this disability well. He had a specific plan to use my disability, is what he said. I wanted the Lord to change His mind. Darn, I was hoping this was not true, and I begged Him to heal me and change His mind. I felt Him using me because I listen to His way of life and live my life the way He would have wanted.

Anything that goes against God's Word is wrong to me—I mean *anything*. Even Satan describes himself as an angel of light (2 Corinthians 11:14). Angels that are good, they always say, "Do not be afraid," in the Bible. They are the good guys and not to be scared. I wonder what they think being portrayed as girly or babies in some pictures. "And we do this so that we may not be outwitted by Satan; we are not ignorant of his designs" (2 Corinthians 2:11). He is tricky and comes to steal, kill, and destroy. I fear others underestimate him. They relish in the power they have over him. "The thief comes only to steal and kill and destroy" (John 10:10).

You know, I found out Satan can even make you think something is from God. Also if he was an angel of light, it has to freak you out due to the fact, in the Bible, angels always say, "Do not be afraid." So if the devil is an angel, he must be scary! Listen, he said it, you could be outwitted by him. The Word says we should resist him. Show me in the Bible where it says get into or pick a fight with him.

> Resist him, (the devil) steadfast in your faith, for you know that your brothers and sisters in all the world are undergoing the same kinds of suffering. And after you have suffered for a little, the God of all grace, who has called you to His eternal glory in Christ, will Himself restore, support, strengthen, and establish you. To Him be the power forever and ever.(1 Peter 5:9–11)

It says *resist* the devil. The book of Mark 16:14–18 says:

> Later he appeared to the eleven themselves as they were sitting at the table; and he upbraided them for their lack of faith and stubbornness, because they had not believed those who saw him after he had risen. And he said to them, "Go into all the world and proclaim the good news to the whole creation. The one who believes and is baptized will be saved; but the one who does not believe will be condemned. And these signs will accompany those who believe: by using my name they will cast out demons; they will speak in new tongues; they will pick on their hands, and if they drink any deadly thing, it will not hurt them; they will lay their hands on the sick.

> Now the serpent was craftier than any other wild animal that the Lord God had made. See he was crafty! He said to the woman, "Did God say, 'You shall not eat from any tree in the garden?'" The woman said to the serpent, "We may eat of the fruit of the trees in the garden; but God said,

'You shall not eat of the fruit of the tree that is in the middle of the garden, nor shall you touch it, or you shall die.'" But the serpent said to the woman, "You will not die; for God knows that when you eat of it your eyes will be opened, and you will be like God, knowing good and evil." So when the woman saw that the tree was good for food, and that it was a delight to the eyes, and that the tree was to be desired to make one wise, she took of its fruit and ate; and she also gave some to her husband, who was with her, and he ate. Then the eyes of both were opened, and they knew that they were naked; and they sewed fig leaves together and made loincloths for themselves. (Genesis 3:1–7)

The devil is cunning, and we can be so duped by him.

You know the devil came into God's presence before? No one really talks about it. This is biblical. He constantly accuses us. I bet I would not be able to handle the greatness of God. According to Scripture, the devil can; others will say that where God is, the devil cannot be. The Scriptures say otherwise.

In the land of Uz there lived a man whose name was Job. This man was blameless and upright; he feared God and shunned evil. He had seven sons and three daughters, and he owned seven thousand sheep, three thousand camels, five hundred yoke of oxen and five hundred donkeys, and had a large number of servants. He was the greatest man among all the people of the East. His sons used to hold feasts in their homes on their birthdays, and they would invite their three sisters to eat and drink with them. When a period of feasting had run its course, Job would make arrangements for them to be purified. Early in the morning he would sacri-

fice a burnt offering for each of them, thinking,
"Perhaps my children have sinned and cursed God
in their hearts." This was Job's regular custom.
One day the angels came to present themselves
before the Lord, and Satan also came with them.
The Lord said to Satan, "Where have you come
from?" Satan answered the Lord, "From roaming
throughout the earth, going back and forth on it.
Then the Lord said to Satan, "Have you considered my servant Job? There is no one on earth like
him; he is blameless and upright, a man who fears
God and shuns evil." "Does Job fear God for nothing?" Satan replied. "Have you not put a hedge
around him and his household and everything he
has? You have blessed the work of his hands, so
that his flocks and herds are spread throughout
the land. But now stretch out your hand and strike
everything he has, and he will surely curse you to
your face." The Lord said to Satan, "Very well,
then, everything he has is in your power, but on
the man himself do not lay a finger." Then Satan
went out from the presence of the Lord. I do not
think about the devil and let God deal with him.
See the devil has access to God. In the book of
Luke, "Simon, Simon! Indeed, Satan has asked for
you, that he may sift you as wheat". (Job 1:6–12)

If you have a disability, you can feel sifted too. I know I do.
Some days, I feel I cannot handle a disability. Satan has to go through
God, and God has all the authority. It gives me some comfort. I love
the saying on Facebook that says, "This is God and I will be handling
your problems." God must think I can handle a lot! I feel so resilient.
Eve was created by God was duped by the devil.

But I am afraid that, as the serpent deceived Eve
by his craftiness, your minds will be led astray

from the simplicity and purity of devotion to Christ. (2 Corinthians 11:3)

The serpent said to the woman, "You surely will not die! "For God knows that in the day you eat from it your eyes will be opened, and you will be like God, knowing good and evil." (Genesis 3:4–5)

He is so tricky. The Scripture in Genesis says he is crafty. I must let God fight my battle against him because he is so crafty. The devil has been sinning from the beginning and has had tons of practice. Even Adam and Eve were duped by the devil and they were made by God. See, resisting the devil is a good idea.

I saw a lot and experienced how people can be. I do not look at the time Jesus comes back as wonderful. I am glad to live one day at a time. I am not the provider. This always means being spiritually ready. I wake up and think immediately about Jesus, and when I lay down, I think of Him. Why I do this is to make sure I am putting Him first, and I feel like with a disability, we must be even more aware the devil wants to take us down. We have a bull's-eye on us as Christians and even more in having a disability. I think others with a disability can easy be led away, especially if they are not healed. Disability makes it so easy to lose heart.

I love ignorant bliss, not sure this is healthy. The day of Christ, when He comes again, many people will suffer and some we might love and want no harm to come to them. We will never know.

A funny story about me doing clinical social work, we had an accrediting organization come and they were to ask questions to the workers. I did much to avoid being asked a question, I was nervous. I made myself aware where they were at all times. I would go to the bathroom to hide or find plants to hide behind. Can you imagine what I looked like, hiding behind plants? I later worked as a case manager who was picked to deal with auditors. I had to answer for others' paperwork. I remember, we had to suck up to them. I thought I could do it. I joked with them and said if they liked the coffee, I made it, and if they did not like the coffee, I did not make it.

Just a thought, when God says, "Gird up your loins like a man," like in the book of Job, it's funny to me. I translate that to, "Suck it up, buttercup!"

I love American history and want to go by to Pikeville, about one hour away, to see the Hatfield's and McCoy's places. I saw the movie on the History Channel. I watched so many shows about ghosts and thought this place was haunted. I carry the mark of Christ and believe there is a devil and demons, (I call thugs) and I believe in angels too. "But it is God who establishes us with you in Christ and has anointed us, by putting his seal on us and giving us his Spirit in our hearts as a first installment, for it is on him that God the Father has set his seal" (2 Corinthians 1:21–22). It is possible there are ghosts. I do not think about them. I let God worry about all that. What I know I must be concerned about is the battery in my chair. What if a ghost tries to take my battery in my chair to manifest? The things I think about! I plan on going. When they all go up in the general store, I won't be able to go due to my wheelchair and the stairs, I refuse to be alone. I am too chicken.

Christians names are written in the Book of Life which the Lord knows what we are dealing with. Bad things happen to good people all the time. I feel I am a good person who some bad things happened to. It may be a surprise to us and something God knew all along. There are many examples in the Bible of someone who had a disability and God knew about it. You might say, "How can this disability be okay with God?" I have learned in my life, there is nothing that has happened that He is not aware of, good or bad.

We are in the Book of Life; there are many scriptures that proves God has a book.

> But now, if you will only forgive their sin—but if not, blot me out of the book that you have written. (Exodus 32:32)

> But now, if you will only forgive their sin—but if not, blot me out of the book that you have written. (Malachi 3:16)

> And all the inhabitants of the earth will wor-
> ship it, everyone whose name has not been writ-
> ten from the foundation of the world in the
> book of life of the Lamb that was slaughtered.
> (Revelations 13:8)

I like it being established in the foundation of the world. This shows that God knows all. One more scripture. "If you conquer, you will be clothed like them in white robes, and I will not blot your name out of the book of life; I will confess your name before my Father and before his angels" (Revelation 3:5).

The name of Jesus holds power. I was taught this from a young age. I washed clothes in the basement as a young girl. Our basement was scary to me; I dreaded it. One time, I was told to get something out of our basement refrigerator and an octopus and squid fell out of the refrigerator on top of me. We had a laundry chute and my clothes were put in it, making me surprised. It scared me. I said, "Jesus!" Not as a bad word, just I guessed Jesus was with me. I was hoping for His help. My mom loves sea food.

Look at Joseph's life and him telling his brothers and his brothers got jealous. Here is the spot in the Bible:

> Joseph had a dream and when he told his broth-
> ers, they hated him even more. He said to them,
> "Please listen to the dream I had. We were tying
> grain into bundles out in the field, and suddenly
> mine stood up. It remained standing while your
> bundles gathered around my bundle and bowed
> down to it."
>
> Then his brothers asked him, "Are you
> going to be our king or rule us?" They hated him
> even more for his dreams and his words.
>
> Then he had another dream, and he told it
> to his brothers. "Listen," he said, "I had another
> dream: I saw the sun, the moon, and 11 stars
> bowing down to me."

When he told his father and his brothers, his father criticized him by asking, "What's this dream you had? Will your mother and I and your brothers come and bow down in front of you?" So his brothers were jealous of him, but his father kept thinking about these things.

His brothers had gone to take care of their father's flocks at Shechem. Israel then said to Joseph, "Your brothers are taking care of the flocks at Shechem. I'm going to send you to them."

Joseph responded, "I'll go."

So Israel said, "See how your brothers and the flocks are doing, and bring some news back to me." Then he sent Joseph away from the Hebron Valley.

When Joseph came to Shechem, a man found him wandering around in the open country. "What are you looking for?" the man asked.

Joseph replied, "I'm looking for my brothers. Please tell me where they're taking care of their flocks."

The man said, "They moved on from here. I heard them say, 'Let's go to Dothan.'" So, Joseph went after his brothers and found them at Dothan.

They saw him from a distance. Before he reached them, they plotted to kill him. They said to each other, "Look, here comes that master dreamer! Let's kill him, throw him into one of the cisterns, and say that a wild animal has eaten him. Then we'll see what happens to his dreams." (Genesis 37:3–20)

We never have to question God or His Word. He sees our whole lives and is working for all of us. Come on, you have questioned God about your disability; I sure have. I look at when God came to Job to argue and show how much God has the power to create and know. I would probably be dead because of God's power.

When I was in high school, I had fun because of my friends and cousins. My cousins and I had the same friends and called the group of girls the Silly Bitches. We would all put a dollar bill in the family car I had, and it filled up our tank. We would do and act funny stuff; for example, we would fill up our car (back then gas was cheap) and tell guys in their cars there would be a party with lots of pretty girls. We would get at least five cars to follow us, and my car would overheat at a party store! The boys would knock on our windows, and we would lock the doors and laugh. We would do stuff like the guys on *Impractical Jokers*.

We even had one SB moon a cop! You know who you are! The funniest was throwing my cousin's shoes in a convertible we did not know. There she was, tilted in a stranger's car at a party store. The stranger came out and poor cousin got yelled at with profanities and asked, "What the hell are you doing!" We all laughed the more he got mad. My cousin tried to explain. The SBs even went to a haunted house and got stuck in the middle. You see, if you were in the middle, you did not get scared first; and if you were in the back, you would get chased with a chain saw. My friend and I fought for the middle spot, we got stuck in the middle and was told to move along. We did worse things we will take to our grave.

We had a major food and water fight. It started out small, and then water was taken out of pools. Eggs and shaving cream were involved. My car got it good; it was so messy, and I forgot my window was cracked and made one of my Silly Bitches roll it up. She got egged in the back. I was not going to go out there. She got messed with, and all we could do was laugh. I had to pick up my mom from work in that car, and there was no way I was going alone. So I took my cousin with me; I was sure I was going to get in trouble. My mom looked at us and then the car and told us to have it cleaned before my dad saw it. She never mentioned it again.

One of our friend from SB thought it was funny to pinch me in sensitive places, like on the upper arms or on the thighs. She pinched me as I was driving and laughed. My cousins were in the back of my little blue Escort and I slammed on my brakes and punched my friend, and then we all laughed. She kept on saying, "I cannot believe you hit me!" I wanted her to stop pinching me so she got punched. I hit the brakes so hard, there were the girls in the back of the car and all I saw was blonde hair flying. We think it is funny today; I got through high school by laughing. Everyone was so serious and negative. We had chapel each day and I had laugh attacks too much. I was told I was rebellious and a spirit of mockery. That made me laugh harder. As Silly Bitches, we even had a girl on the roof of my cousin's car. And she said help, and we honked the horn and laughed. We were such bad kids and never knew or thought it.

I was a bad teen and would never let my parents know what I did; they would kill me. I went on a senior trip to Disney World in Florida. And my friend had cigarettes, and I told her I would smoke with her. We were high up, and we were afraid of setting the sprinklers off and getting caught, so we stupidly took out our window, we were high up. We took the whole thing out and leaned it indoor. I did so many dumb things. One thing I do not regret is when we went to the ride at Disney called the Haunted Manichean SP, and my class went in an elevator and they turned off the lights, I screamed like I was afraid, and others would get mad and said I was immature. My friends and I laughed and laughed harder when others got mad.

I think I got my sense of humor from my dad; he was always cracking jokes. There was a time my mom asked me to grab her a cup of ice water; I made it and gave it to my dad. He would say, "Thanks, and now make one for your mom." He was funny. Whenever he would burp, he would say, "Better out than in." He told me he was proud of me before he got sick. That meant a lot to me.

In high school, my friend and I would imitate what we saw on *Saturday Night Live*. It was during English class and we were not the best students. There was a time we had to read *Macbeth* out loud, and the most popular guy was sitting in front of us and one friend was sitting next to him. We decided to have our friend in front of us put her hand gently on his leg when it was his time to read. Our friend did it! We laughed, and he laughed.

I had a small class of twenty-five people, and I was a class clown. There was another friend, and I got kicked out of class to the hallway for laughing. The teacher said, "I can hear you laughing in the hallway!" Our teacher got the principal. He was not mad and told me all about Asbury University and he said his son went there. To me, high school was fun.

I read a scripture in some devotions I find hard. It must be important because it is in the Bible. I hate to be disabled.

Is your fruit stinky?

> By contrast, the fruit of the Spirit is love, joy, peace, patience, kindness, generosity, faithfulness, gentleness, and self-control. There is no law against such things. And those who belong to Christ Jesus have crucified the flesh with its passions and desires. If we live by the Spirit, let us also be guided by the Spirit. Let us not become conceited, competing against one another, envying one another. (Galatians 5:22–26)

Love, are you kidding? Love all? Come on, this is just hard!

> And hope does not disappoint us, because God's love has been poured into our hearts through the Holy Spirit that has been given to us. (Romans 5:5)

> Now concerning food sacrificed to idols: we know that "all of us possess knowledge." Knowledge puffs up, but love builds up. (1 Corinthians 8:1)

> But showing steadfast love to the thousandth generation of those who love me and keep my commandments. (Exodus 20:6)

Love comes from God and builds up. We are called to love and follow him. We have to love others.

Does your life with a disability produce good works and glory to God? Take time and really think about it. Sometimes life following God can mean we, at times, do without. What does your life look like to others? Do all areas of your life bring light? We cannot pick and choose what part of our lives do good or glorify God; just because you have a disability does not mean you can pick or choose.

Living for God can be different from the world and what the world sees as important. Our number 1 thing about our lives show we live for God.

Joy with disability—this is so hard! Is there such a thing? It feels like some of my joy has been taken away. Since I do not live totally relying on my changing feelings. Let us see what the Word of God says about the fruit.

Let us begin with joy:

> Then he said to them, "Go your way, eat the fat and drink sweet wine and send portions of them to those for whom nothing is prepared, for this day is holy to our Lord; and do not be grieved, for the joy of the Lord is your strength." (Nehemiah 8:10)

> I have said these things to you so that my joy may be in you, and that your joy may be complete. (John 15:11)

> Very truly, I tell you, you will weep and mourn, but the world will rejoice; you will have pain, but your pain will turn into joy. (John 16:20)

If Jesus says, "Very truly, I tell you," it means business and it is so important to know. Joy is something to strive for. The way I live is, one day at a time; and I find joy in something each day, like my husband, kids, and dog. I love to do puzzles and watch television. I cannot focus on what I cannot do and have to focus on what I can do. I have to practice this.

Peace is next. "For he is our peace; in his flesh he has made both groups into one and has broken down the dividing wall, that is, the hostility between us" (Ephesians 2:1). This next verse is really important for those of us with disability.

> And the peace of God, which surpasses all understanding, will guard your hearts and your minds in Christ Jesus. (Philippians 4:20)

> Let them turn away from evil and do good let them seek peace and pursue it. (1 Peter 3:11)

What I see from the Bible is that peace comes from God and we need to pursue it. I think my husband, Tim, is good in this area. He is one who is ready to have peace. His strength is he is such a peacemaker. "Blessed are the peacemakers, for they will be called children of God" (Matthew 5:9). He will never say it. I admire him for it. In fact, if he gets in an argument with another, he is probably right. I swear, he is the nicest person I have ever known.

Patience is very important for us with a disability. It is a forced trait and we have to fake it all the time. When you are disabled, you have no choice. Our caregivers want to help and do things different than you. This is a hard lesson to learn. You have to let them in order to put their feelings above your own.

> As God's chosen ones, holy and beloved, clothe yourselves with compassion, kindness, humility, meekness, and patience. (Colossians 3:12)

> Be patient, therefore, beloved until the coming of the Lord. The farmer waits for the precious crop from the earth, being patient with it until it receives the early and the late rains. You also must be patient. Strengthen your hearts, for the coming of the Lord is near. (James 5:7–8)

If you have a disability, you have most likely suffered. When my body got hooked on pain medicine, I went through withdrawals.

I suffered greatly and could not stand it. The pain of withdrawal is worse to me than labor, kidney stones, or bowel surgery. I could not stand it; it was a pain, impossible to sit still. The air even hurt. I begged God to do something about my suffering. He did nothing. It was hard for my family to see, and I knew it had to be hard for God to watch. God did not take the painkillers. He did not make the change. I think God gets a bad rap on not answering our prayer like we want. Just because we have a disability does not give us a free pass to not reap what we sow. "Do not be deceived; God is not mocked, for you reap whatever you sow" (Galatians 6:7). I wanted it to all go away. I do not have that patience during suffering down; God will have to help me learn this.

Kindness is the next fruit.

> Put away from you all bitterness and wrath and anger and wrangling and slander, together with all malice, and be kind to one another, tender-hearted, forgiving one another, as God in Christ has forgiven you. (Ephesians 4:31–32)

> But when the goodness and loving kindness of God our Savior appeared, he saved us, not because of any works of righteousness that we had done, but according to his mercy, through the water of rebirth and renewal by the Holy Spirit. This Spirit he poured out on us richly through Jesus Christ our Savior, so that, having been justified by his grace, we might become heirs according to the hope of eternal life. (Titus 3:4–7)

We should be kind to one another. This does not mean have a bad relationship with others. I have cut out people I think are not healthy in my life. This is seen as I am having no forgiveness. Having to deal with a disability and all that goes with it can be tiring. I keep out of my life any negative force or person. I am just too tired. I have to reserve my strength for my husband and kids. Having a disability, I get sleepy more so now.

Generosity is next. "It is well with those who deal generously and lend, who conduct their affairs with justice" (Psalms 112:5).

Faithfulness is my strong area. I have been optimistic even with my circumstances going bad. I live for heaven and not for this world. According to *Dictionary Online, faithfulness* is defined as "loyal, true, constant, steadfast, staunch."

These adjectives mean adhering firmly and devotedly to someone or something that elicits or demands one's fidelity.

- *Faithful* and *loyal* both suggest undeviating attachment, though loyal applies more often to political allegiance: *a faithful employee; a loyal citizen.*
- *True* implies steadiness, sincerity, and reliability: *remained true to her innermost beliefs.*
- *Constant* stresses uniformity and invariability: *"But I am constant as the northern star"* (Shakespeare).
- *Steadfast* implies fixed, unswerving loyalty: *a steadfast ally.*
- *Staunch* even more strongly suggests unshakable attachment or allegiance: *a staunch supporter of the cause* the quality of being faithful."

"Hezekiah did this throughout all Judah; he did what was good and right and faithful before the Lord his God. And every work that he undertook in the service of the house of God, and in accordance with the law and the commandments, to seek his God, he did with all his heart; and he prospered" (2 Cornicles 31:20–21).

God is always watching us.

> You are the Lord, the God who chose Abram and brought him out of Ur of the Chaldeans and gave him the name Abraham; and you found his heart faithful before you, and made with him a covenant to give to his descendants the land of the Canaanite, the Hittite, the Amorite, the

> Perizzite, the Jebusite, and the Girgashite; and you have fulfilled your promise, for you are righteous. (Nehemiah 9:7–8)

> Whoever is faithful in a very little is faithful also in much; and whoever is dishonest in a very little is dishonest also in much. If then you have not been faithful with the dishonest whether who will entrust to you the true riches? And if you have not been faithful with what belongs to another, who will give you what is your own? (Luke 6:10–12)

Gentleness is next. My friends, if anyone is detected in a transgression, you who have received the Spirit should restore such a one in a spirit of gentleness (Galatians 6:1–10).

"Come to me, all you that are weary and are carrying heavy burdens, and I will give you rest. Take my yoke upon you and learn from me; for I am gentle and humble in heart, and you will find rest for your souls. For my yoke is easy, and my burden is light" (Matthew 11:28–30).

Even Jesus was gentle. It is good to know that we do not walk alone. Jesus is with us even when we go through bed circumstances. I always say, "It is better go through the bad times with God than not."

> I therefore, the prisoner in the Lord, beg you to lead a life worthy of the calling to which you have been called, with all humility and gentleness, with patience. (Ephesians 4:1–3)

> Some days later when Felix came with his wife Drusilla, who was Jewish, he sent for Paul and heard him speak concerning faith in Christ Jesus. And as he discussed justice, self-control, and the coming judgment, Felix became frightened and said, "Go away for the present; when I get an opportunity I will summon you." (Acts 24:24–25)

CHAPTER 3

I've read this scripture and I find it hard. "My brother and sisters where you face trials of any kind, consider it nothing be joy. Because you know that the testing of your faith produces endurance and endurance, and let endurance have its full effect, so that you that may be mature and complete, lacking in nothing" (James 1:2–4). I find no joy in being disabled and the words *testing* or *joy*. We are in good company; even Abraham was tested. It is never talked about.

Abraham was the great father of a multitude of nations, and no one has been found like him in glory. He kept the law of the Highest and entered into a covenant with Him; he certified the covenant in his flesh, and when he was tested, he proved faithful. The whole chapter of Sirach 44:20 talks about some of the famous people in the Bible. Abraham was tested, but I am not sure how. You know, testing of any kind stinks. What if my disability is a test? I wrote mine, not yours. I have no idea. I love the movie *Evan Almighty*; he built an ark and he was getting ready for a flood. His wife said to Evan, it could be a flood of ideas, Evan said, "I would be so pissed."

I hate to be this way. However, Tim continues to love me. I am amazed at all he does. Disability is devastating and traumatic; we have to go through it with God. It is hard for those of us to not be like we were before. I see on television, preachers have a prayer cloth or a stone form Jesus's tomb. I bet! Also holy water. I could get a stone from my driveway or water out of the tap and call it whatever.

You may feel desperate with having your disability. Nothing we can do can make it all okay, life is hard. It can be hard, and we all have problems. It is not easy to suffer. We want to run from it or avoid it. I was just like that. I did not say you have an unknown sin. I have no idea. I say to pray; what have you got to lose? I have no idea when prayers will or will not work out our way. All I know is to pray about it. Who is to say that our prayers are working or not? As we have a disability, who says we get healed or not?

Do you realize the same God who we have in us is the same God could who make our bodies work right now? Us with disability right now are called to live a deeper relationship with him. For reasons we are not right now, we will never know. If it is for us to not be healed right now, only He knows. A deeper trust must be. Come on, we need to have God to deal with disability. I love that Garth Brooks song "Unanswered Prayers." I saw him in concert with a friend in 1994.

Look at St. Paul's life. This guy had been blind, prisoned, ship-wrecked, and flogged. Come on, he had so many things bad happen to him in his life.

> But I wish to boast (St. Paul), I will not be a fool, for I will be speaking the truth. But I refrain from it, for no one may think better of me than what is seen in me or heard from me, even considering the exceptional character of the revelations. Therefore, to keep me from being too elated, a thorn was given me in the flesh, a massager of Satan to torment me, from keeping me from being too elated. Three times I appealed to the Lord about this, for it to leave me, but He said to me, "My grace is sufficient for you, for power is made perfect in weakness." So, I will boast all the more gladly of my weakness, so that the power of Christ may dwell in me. Therefore, I am content with weaknesses, insults, harnesses, persecutions, and calamities for the sake of Christ, for whatever I am weak, then I am strong. (2 Corinthians 12:6–10)

Wow, amazing, right? To say that, and for reasons St. Paul can't understand, the Lord will not take away his problem or thorn in his flesh. Do not forget, it says a messenger from Satan, a thug (what I call demons) most likely. A messenger from Satan? How can this be? This is Paul we are talking about. You know, the guy who wrote much of the New Testament letters. He must have really trusted and waited in God.

Bad comes to us all, our disability is bad. I look at all that happened to Joseph, Jacob's son, and bad came to them both. Come on, he thought his son died a violent death. Abraham's grandson, Abraham, he was a friend to God and he had hard times too.

I think the ultimate insult came to Samuel. Look, "When Samuel became old, he made his sons judges over Israel. The name of his firstborn son was Joel, and the name of his second, Abijah; they were judges in Beer-Sheba. Yet his sons did not follow in his ways but turned aside after gain; they took bribes and perverted justice" (1 Samuel 8). That had to be hard, kid troubles are some of the worst.

I saw some of the *Grammys* and I love to see the outfits on the red carpet. I was taken aback that the winners would thank God. I was so shocked because they do not know what they are saying. "I want to thank God for giving me a gift and creating me." What do they think? "I want to thank God for my raunchy video and music." I kept on thinking, *Stop talking, you are going to make it worse!* I got really upset and turned off when they tried to portray a pregnant girl as our Mother Mary. Come on, there is no comparison at all. I felt horrified. We are comparing ourselves now to the Mother of God. I would be afraid.

We get to fellowship with Jesus if we live our lives for Him, not just on Sundays at church. In the Bible, it says ask whatever you wish and it will be done. I did not get healed and have a broken body and I have asked tons of time for God to make my disability go away. I get nothing. Crickets. I do not know why, I live my life "right in His sight."

It is a very good thing that the Holy Spirit intercedes for us. Sometimes we cannot understand the hard times (having a disability) and have a deeper prayer that only the Holy Spirit knows what we need; right now, as you are, having asked God to get you through the hard times. Sometimes we just say, "Help me God." God is always working for our good while we are in these broken bodies and the hard times. There are so much promises you can look up in your Bible. My whole point is, God loves us and is not mad at us.

My devotions lead me to 1 Samuel and Hannah's story. She poured her heart to God, looking like she was drunk. Sometimes we get what we cried out to God, and sometimes, we do not get what we cried to God for. My point is, she cried out to God and it is something we can do. What do you have to lose? Here is the story of Hannah.

There was a certain man of Ramathaim, a Zuphite from the hill country of Ephraim, whose name was Elkanah son of Jeroham son of Elihu son of Tohu son of Zuph, an Ephraimite. He had two wives; the name of the one was Hannah, and the name of the other Peninnah. Peninnah had children, but Hannah had no children.

Now this man used to go up year by year from his town to worship and to sacrifice to the Lord of hosts at Shiloh, where the two sons of Eli, Hophni and Phinehas, were priests of the Lord. On the day when Elkanah sacrificed, he would give portions to his wife Peninnah and to all her sons and daughters; but to Hannah he gave a double portion, because he loved her, though the Lord had closed her womb. Her rival used to provoke her severely, to irritate her, because the Lord had closed her womb. So it went on year by year; as often as she went up to the house of the Lord, she used to provoke her. Therefore, Hannah wept and would not eat. Her husband Elkanah said to her, "Hannah, why do you weep? Why do you not eat? Why is your heart sad? Am I not more to you than ten sons?"

After they had eaten and drunk at Shiloh, Hannah rose and presented herself before the Lord. Now Eli the priest was sitting on the seat beside the doorpost of the temple of the Lord. She was deeply distressed and prayed to the Lord

and wept bitterly. She made this vow: "O Lord
of hosts, if only you will look on the misery of
your servant, and remember me, and not forget
your servant, but will give to your servant a male
child, then I will set him before you as a Nazirite
until the day of his death. He shall drink neither
wine nor intoxicants, and no razor shall touch
his head."

As she continued praying before the Lord,
Eli observed her mouth. Hannah was praying
silently; only her lips moved, but her voice was
not heard; therefore, Eli thought she was drunk.
So Eli said to her, "How long will you make a
drunken spectacle of yourself? Put away your
wine." But Hannah answered, "No, my lord, I am
a woman deeply troubled; I have drunk neither
wine nor strong drink, but I have been pouring
out my soul before the Lord. Do not regard your
servant as a worthless woman, for I have been
speaking out of my great anxiety and vexation
all this time." Then Eli answered, "Go in peace;
the God of Israel grant the petition you have
made to him." And she said, "Let your servant
find favor in your sight." Then the woman went
to her quarters, ate and drank with her husband,
and her countenance was sad no longer.

They rose early in the morning and worshiped before the Lord; then they went back to
their house at Ramah. Elkanah knew his wife
Hannah, and the Lord remembered her. In due
time Hannah conceived and bore a son. She
named him Samuel, for she said, "I have asked
him of the Lord." (1 Samuel 1)

On an unrelated note, I think heaven might have wine (Luke 22).

The Advent season is here, and we prepare our hearts for God coming in the flesh. A baby and Father. The story of John the Baptist's parents' interests me. Remember, they were past child bearing years (Luke 1:7). But they had no children because Elizabeth was barren and both were getting on in years. An angel appeared to Zechariah and told him he would have son named John.

> Then there appeared to him an angel of the Lord, standing at the right side of altar of incense When Zechariah saw him, he was terrified; fear overwhelmed him (I would be afraid too), But the angel said to him, "Do not be afraid (sure), Zechariah, for your prayer has been heard. Your wife Elizabeth will bear you a son, and you will name him John. You will have great joy and gladness, and many will rejoice at his birth, for he will be great in the sight of the Lord, He must never drink wine or drink; many people of Israel to the Lord their God. With the Spirit and the power of Elijah he will go before Him, to turn the hearts of parents to their children, and the disobedient to the wisdom of the righteous, to make ready a people prepared for the Lord. Zechariah said to the angel, "How will know this to be? For I am an old man, and my wife is getting on in years." The angel replied, "I am Gabriel, I stand in the presence of God, and I have been sent to you and to bring you the good news. But now, because you did not believe my words, which will be fulfilled in their time, you will become mute, unable to speak, until the day those things occur." (Luke 1:11–25)

If you read the rest of the story, you will find out he gets his voice back and John the Baptist was born. A little extreme, don't ya think! The guy was given a disability of not talking due to his unbelief. Now do not freak out on me. God just does not just hand out disabilities. He takes our disabilities and makes some good come out of them. This passage explains we all are heard and His ways are not our ways. How could having a disability be okay with God? I chalk it up to, I don't know.

I love history and was watching the History channel and saw the mystery behind the Nativity scene. Now do not worry, I do not believe everything on the Internet or television. The birth of Jesus had to hurt. Can you imagine being pregnant and having contractions on a donkey and no room at an inn? It was really dark and foreboding. Mary and Joseph had to escape because King Herod had all the children up to two killed.

Herod saw that he had been tricked by the wise men, he was infuriated, and he sent and killed all the children in and around Bethlehem who were two years old or under, according to the time that he had learn from the wise men. Then was fulfilled what had been spoken through the ages through the profit Jeremiah: "A voice was heard in Ramah, wailing and loud lamentation, Rachel weeping for her children; she refuses to be consoled, because they are no more." (Mathew 2:16–18)

It is already dark for me. Children killed. It had to be so hard for all the parents. If we were in that horrible predicament, we would be so, so sad. "And she gave birth to her firstborn Son and wrapped Him in bands of cloth, and laid Him in a manger, because there was no place for them in the inn" (Luke 2:7).

Now do not forget they not only were fleeing but angels came to them. I am sure this was all traumatic. We can forget these were real people. They later got gifts from the wise men and what they gave must have freaked them out as parents.

> On entering the house, they (Wise men) saw the child with Mary his mother; and they knelt down and paid Him homage. Then, opening their treasure chests, they offered Him gifts of gold, frankincense. And myrrh. And having been warned in a dream not to return to Herod, they left for their own country by another road. (Matthew 2:11–12)

This not good. Listen, the child got gold because He was a king and kings had lots of gold. He got frankincense to get ready for His burial, and myrrh was an incense used for the tabernacle. I am sure these were odd presents to get. Who would ever want to know their son is going to die and get gifts tell you about it? Foreboding and dark.

It is Advent and so many specials on television, and I saw one that they were singing hymns. I thought they had no idea what they were singing about. They did for Christmastime and for entertainment. They were singing traditional hymns, not really knowing what they were singing.

Our church, St. Luke's, is going to have a healing-for-the-sick service the next Sunday. I was leaving church and shook the father's hand and told him I wanted in on that action, the action meaning laying hands on and anointing with oil. I cannot tell you the many times I was prayed over in the past years.

Today as I am writing this, it has been many years with disability. It is my anniversary of the day I was paralyzed. It is harder on those that love me. All who love me are being sensitive about it. I know it really messed our family up. I do my best to not think of it. We had no choice and had to create a new normal. You see, I have had many years to deal with it. Do not get me wrong, I hate having a disability. I never had any healing, not once. I used to get jealous of those who got healed and wondered why I did not get healed. Especially in the Bible or just by association. I am sure you and your caregivers feel the same. I think my strength is faith; I have always had it. I used to say to God, "Why not me?" I now am happy to say it is good when anyone gets healed but honestly still wonder, *Why not me?* I am not the type to question or doubt God. I am too afraid for a sign or to put Him to a test.

It is now Sunday, and we had a healing service at Mass. My oldest, Grace, cried; I wanted to hug her and let her know I am okay. I think all were hoping I would get healed right there. See, I got prayed for and anointed so many times but not healed. Was it for nothing?

> Are any among you sick? They should call for elders of the church and have them pray over them, anointing them with oil in the name of the Lord. The prayer of the faith will save the sick, and the Lord will raise them up; and anyone who has committed sins shall be forgiven. Therefore, confess your sins to one another, and pray for one another, so that you may be healed. The prayer of the righteous is powerful and effective. (James 5:14–16)

This is where I think others think we have a big sin. I must be missing something because He is perfect.

> This God—His ways are perfect; the promise of the Lord proves true; He is a shield for all who take refuge in Him. (Psalms 18:30)

> Be perfect, therefore, your heavenly Father is perfect. (Matthew 5:48)

Remember, you will get healing on earth or in heaven. You are unable to have control over what others say. Those that know you know your character. I wait to be healed in heaven or here. Did you forget God is King? You don't mess with God or His angels.

I am too chicken; why do angels get an image where they are displayed as girls or a baby? God was not surprised that Zechariah got mute. By the way, being mute is a disability. Our disability does not surprise God.

I told the father at our church that I wanted in on that action whether I am healed or not. I do not think he ever heard that before. I was being honest and told him what I was thinking. I know when others pray and do not see healing, they could be discouraged and feel like their prayers did not work. I say, get that negative thought out of your head and accept His ways are just not ours. So you get prayed over and prayed for tons of times. You have nothing and you are right where you started before you got prayed for. This is the hard part of doing what you know to do—pray. I still stand on God's Word.

> Are any among you suffering? They should pray. Are any cheerful? They should sing songs of praise. Area any among you sick? They should call for the elders of the church and have them pray over them and anointing them with oil in the name of the Lord. He prayers of faith will save the sick, and the Lord will raise them up; and anyone who has committed sins will be forgiven. Therefore, confess your sins to one another, and pray for one another, so that you may be healed. The prayer of the righteous is powerful and effective. (James 5:13-26)

> Then the Lord said, "I have observed the misery of my people who are in Egypt; I have heard their cry on account of their taskmasters. Indeed, I know their suffering." (Exodus 3:7)

Disability can take years away. "Because their shame was double and dishonor was proclaimed as their lot, therefore they shall possess a double portion; everlasting joy shall be theirs" (Isaiah 61:7). I still wait for my double for my troubles.

What good can come from having a disability? I have been embarrassed so many times and survived at times when I thought I would never survive. I thought I had pretty feet but my bedsores freaked someone out. A guy took off my socks at the hospital and said he just could not deal with my feet today. He was lucky Tim did not hear that. I could not respond because my speech was so bad. He was lucky I could not move or I would have let him have it!

I can get up in front of others and speak with a speech problem and it will not matter to me. If you knew me before my injury, you know I was not able to speak in a large crowd. I do now because now, I have been embarrassed so many times. I am sure if you have a disability, embarrassment comes with it. I think, *What else can happen to me?*

I am writing this book with God's help. Do you know I am typing with two fingers and I do not hurt? I pray before I type; God has other plans for me, plans for me with a disability. Just when I am thinking I am done with writing this book, He floods my mind with ideas and scriptures He wants. Sometimes I wake up at night, when all are sleeping, and I get ideas for the book and I can no longer write so God must help me remember. It is like water on a rock. I cannot explain it any other way. He has compassion for disabled and caregivers. He knows how we feel. I wake up each day, thinking, *This day I could be healed.* I am always hopeful even when no changes ever happen. I am still the same.

I asked God's to help me manage today. I asked God to help me live with disability and wait for His healing. I wish all the time I had no disability. So I only do what I know I can do—pray. I will say it again, when you do not know what to do, do what you know to do. It is so important to know and have a life of prayer. Talk to God, He gets it; let Jesus be your example. He prayed.

After He dismissed the crowds, He went up the mountain by Himself to pray. When evening came, He was there alone. (Matthew 14:23)

Then Jesus went with them to a place called Gethsemane, and He said to the disciples "Sit here while I do over there and pray." (Matthew 26:36)

I think this is the reason we do nothing but focus on God from noon to 3:00 p.m. on Good Friday. We did this when we were little kids, and my parents made sure we followed the tradition of nothing from noon to 3:00 p.m. I have my kids do the same.

"Then Jesus said, 'Father forgive them; for they do not know what they are doing'" (Luke 23:34). He was in great pain and prayed anyway. There on the cross, He was feeling forsaken by God. Even Jesus was feeling forsaken a similar way we can feel in having a disability, sound familiar? No one talks about Jesus feeling forsaken on the cross. Others want to tie up God in a box and take it out occasionally. God knows exactly how we feel. If you have a disability or are taking care of a loved one, you feel a little forsaken by God. When I was a clinical social worker, I would have to ask those I counseled how they felt. If they said, "I don't know?", I would make them guess so I had something to work with. Protestant or Catholic, we both serve the same God. I have heard before that Catholics are going to hell and too ridged or planned. Let us not forget, others will try to heal you and feel your disability is the result of sin. Some people will pray for you, but you must realize, someone's view or opinion should not matter. They will think their opinion matters or is important and yours does not matter. Those of us who have a disability have bigger fish to fry. I just let them think and feel whatever, even when it is bad.

Catholic or Protestant does not mean that it is the better way of worshipping God. I hear so much that we pray to saints; we *ask them to pray* for us, see the difference? We ask others to pray for us like on Facebook. Why is it any different? I treat God like a King and He deserves to be treated at church and throughout the week. This is so important to me. I try to live my life *each* day, not just on Sundays. I must live my life for Him, especially being disabled. This means I must learn to do without things, but I get godly stuff like having Him be with me always, even my circumstance stink. I like communion each week with wine more than once a month with grape juice. Jesus says, "In remembrance of Him."

"Then he took a loaf of bread, and when he had given thanks, he broke it and gave it to them, saying, 'This is my body, which is given for you. Do this in remembrance of me'" (Luke 22:19).

Our broken bodies can still be temples of God; it is not hopeless.

"Or do you not know that your body is a temple of the Holy Spirit within you, which you have from God, and that you are not your own? For you were bought with a price; therefore, glorify God in your body" (1 Corinthians 6:19–20).

How can our broken bodies glorify God? Sometimes you think, *The Scripture is not for me.* You may feel you have a set rules for you. Scripture is all for you, and you don't have a different set of rules for you. You might be broken. God wants us to lead a life disabled to glorify Him as you feel you are suffering a disability. Glorify?

The following are from me searching for what *glory* means in the Bible. What I discovered is that "glory" is most often and action. Glory: Something you do.

When used as a verb, *glory* means to put confidence in and boast about or praise something. This may be used in the sense of glorying in God or Christ, which the Bible portrays as a good thing, or to glory in yourself or your nature which the Bible portrays as sinful.

There are twenty different variations of Hebrew, Aramaic, and Greek words commonly translated as "glory" in English Bibles. Depending on the context, *glory* can be used in several different ways. Most of them are associated with ascribing splendor and majesty to God, but glory is also used as a verb, as in, "to glory in something." The most common use of the word *glory* in the Bible is to describe the splendor, holiness, and majesty of God. Glory, in this sense, is often associated with a person experiencing God's presence in a tangible way. When used this way, the word *glory* conveys a sense of heavy dignity.

One example of this is recorded in 2 Chronicles 5. According to the biblical account, God's glory filled the newly constructed temple. This was experienced tangibly by those around who saw a cloud fill the temple. This cloud, which signified God's glory and presence, temporarily prevented the priests from conducting their duties.

I got the following from the Internet, and I feel I could not have said it better:

> Under the Old Covenant, the temple was the house of God, the place of prayer for His people, the children of Israel. The temple had three compartments, one of which was the Holy of Holies, and it held the presence of God! Amazingly, now our renewed and sanctified spirit is the place where His presence dwells!
>
> Under the New Covenant, the apostle Paul tells us that God's presence is now a mystery

revealed, which is of Christ in us, "the Hope of glory" (see Colossians 1:27).

Because of the union you now have with Christ, you can be close to God because you are God's living temple. You are indwelt by the Holy Spirit, a building still under construction, but nonetheless His house, His tabernacle. Paul goes to great length in encouraging us to live a holy life because we are the temple of God.

Whereas the children of Israel had to go to a specific place to offer their worship with detailed instructions, we have the incredible privilege of worshiping God anywhere and at any time. Therefore, we can be called a house of prayer."

We all have to suffer sometime, and with disability, we have suffered. We all have to suffer sometime. In the book of Judith, her people, the Israelites, needed to have water. They were faint and people were literally dying, young an old (suffering). Their enemies, the Assyrians, hogged all the water well for themselves. She cried out to God and pretended to be on the Assyrian side. Now the following is one of my favorite parts:

> She removed the sackcloth she had been wearing, took off her widow's garments, bathed her body with water, and anointed herself with precious ointment. She combed her hair, put on a tiara, and dressed herself in the festive attire that she used to wear while her husband Manasseh was living. She put sandals on her feet, and put on her anklets, bracelets, rings, earrings, and all her other jewelry. Thus, she made herself very beautiful, to entice the eyes of all the men who might see her. She gave her maid a skin of wine and a flask of oil, and filled a bag with roasted grain, dried fig cakes, and fine bread then she wrapped

SELAH: COFFEE WITH GOD

up all her dishes and gave them to her to carry. (Judith 10:3–5)

She dressed up and got her fashion on. Not only did she dress up, she bought food! I have always learned, a way to a man is through his stomach, right?. If she was not an Israelite, I would swear she was Sicilian. She used her looks too.

When Judith came into the presence of Holofernes and his servants, they all marveled at the beauty of her face. She prostrated herself and did obeisance to him, but his slaves raised her up. (Judith 10:23)

Then Judith came in and lay down. Holofernes' heart was ravished with her and his passion was aroused, for he had been waiting for an opportunity to seduce her from the day he first saw her. So Holofernes said to her, "Have a drink and be merry with us!" Judith said, "I will gladly drink, my lord, because today is the greatest day in my whole life." Then she took what her maid had prepared and ate and drank before him. Holofernes was greatly pleased with her, and drank a great quantity of wine, much more than he had ever drunk in any one day since he was born. (Judith 12:16–20)

Holofernes the jerk! He was planning to seduce her all along.

On the fourth day Holofernes held a banquet for his personal attendants only and did not invite any of his officers. He said to Bagoas, the eunuch who had charge of his personal affairs, "Go and persuade the Hebrew woman who is in your care to join us and to eat and drink with us. For it would be a disgrace if we let such a woman go

71

without having intercourse with her. If we do not seduce her, she will laugh at us." (Judith 12:10–12)

A disgrace to not have intercourse with him! Who does he think he is? God's gift to woman, pleeeaase! He was planning to seduce her but was so drunk he fell asleep.

When evening came, his slaves quickly withdrew. Bagoas closed the tent from outside and shut out the attendants from his master's presence. They went to bed, for they all were weary because the banquet had lasted so long. But Judith was left alone in the tent, with Holofernes stretched out on his bed, for he was dead drunk.

Now Judith had told her maid to stand outside the bedchamber and to wait for her to come out, as she did on the other days; for she said she would be going out for her prayers. She had said the same thing to Bagoas. So everyone went out, and no one, either small or great, was left in the bedchamber. Then Judith, standing beside his bed, said in her heart, "O Lord God of all might, look in this hour on the work of my hands for the exaltation of Jerusalem. Now indeed is the time to help your heritage and to carry out my design to destroy the enemies who have risen up against us."

She went up to the bedpost near Holofernes' head, and took down his sword that hung there. She came close to his bed, took hold of the hair of his head, and said, "Give me strength today, O Lord God of Israel!" Then she struck his neck twice with all her might, and cut off his head. Next, she rolled his body off the bed and pulled down the canopy from the posts. Soon afterward she went out and gave Holofernes' head to her maid, who placed it in her food bag., sucks to be her maid).

Then the two of them went out together, as they were accustomed to do for prayer. They passed through the camp, circled around the valley, and went up the mountain to Bethulia, and came to its gates. From a distance Judith called out to the sentries at the gates, "Open, open the gate! God, our God, is with us, still showing his power in Israel and his strength against our enemies, as he has done today!"

When the people of her town heard her voice, they hurried down to the town gate and summoned the elders of the town. They all ran together, both small and great, for it seemed unbelievable that she had returned. They opened the gate and welcomed them. Then they lit a fire to give light and gathered around them. Then she said to them with a loud voice, "Praise God, O praise him! Praise God, who has not withdrawn his mercy from the house of Israel but has destroyed our enemies by my hand this very night!"

Then she pulled the head out of the bag and showed it to them, and said, "See here, the head of Holofernes, the commander of the Assyrian army, and here is the canopy beneath which he lay in his drunken stupor. The Lord has struck him down by the hand of a woman. As the Lord lives, who has protected me in the way I went, I swear that it was my face that seduced him to his destruction, and that he committed no sin with me, to defile and shame me."

All the people were greatly astonished. They bowed down and worshiped God, and said with one accord, "Blessed are you our God, who have this day humiliated the enemies of your people."

Then Uzziah said to her, "O daughter, you are blessed by the Most High God above all other women on earth; and blessed be the Lord God, who created the heavens and the earth, who has guided you to cut off the head of the leader of our enemies. Your praise will never depart from the hearts of those who remember the power of God. May God grant this to be a perpetual honor to you, and may he reward you with blessings, because you risked your own life when our nation was brought low, and you averted our ruin, walking in the straight path before our God." And all the people said, "Amen. Amen." (Judith 13)

He was asleep on his bed, then she cut off his head off and put it in a bag. What I think we can't miss in Judith's book of the Bible is the fact the people still got it bad. They still had it hard, they thirsted and even some died. You can still have hard times at the same time God is working.

I have a funny Sicilian story about me canning. If you are a good Sicilian, then you can. I cannot do it now, and Grace will be taught how to can by her Kentucky mother-in-law. That's what they do in Kentucky. I used to can all the time and liked it. The very first time I canned my Sicilian sauce, I had no funnel. So I decide to use a paper plate a make a funnel. This was my downfall, bad idea. I canned my sauce, and when I tasted it, it tasted off. The coating on the paper plates melted off in my sauce. All my hard work, tons off cans too. At the time, we lived in a small town and word of what I did got out. The following Sunday, I got five funnels.

True story: Before Tim was a guy I dated and he came over for dinner and we made homemade sauce to eat on pasta. He said, while we were eating, his mom's jar sauce was better. I was a good Sicilian who made sauce, and the recipe was from my dad's father from Sicily. He said a jar sauce was better. Who says that? He could have lied and said it was good, why? I was horrified because my family all looked up in shock and did not say a word. Crickets. I thought, *Now he did it*. It was an insult. Thank the Lord I broke up with him. I tell my girls that a guy has to fit in a family. I told them, "You should be free to do whatever, whenever you want. It is mandatory to be yourself." I am so comfortable with Tim.

Funny story, there was a time we went to my godmother's house and my grandma lived there. My aunt made some pasta for us and later made my grandma American macaroni and cheese; she never had it before. My grandma said it was so good and asked what is was. My aunt told her and said she kept it for when her grandchildren came. It was fun watching her try it; my grandma said it was good and told my aunt that she cooked the noodles too long. Tim and I held in our laughter and my aunt too. Tim and I just kept our heads down and pretended it was never said.

When I was pregnant with my youngest, Hope, the smell of any onion or coffee made me sick. I like them normally; I could stand the smell of them. I would be a good Sicilian and have my pasta once a week. I would have Tim make my sauce and use onion powder while I yelled instructions from a different room. True story. You know what we Sicilians call the trinity of cooking? It is olive oil, garlic, and onions. True!

I used to be able to write. I am no longer able to do so, however, I wrote in my Bible, long ago, what being in the valley was like. The valley meaning where all bad happens, bad circumstances. We all have been in a valley, a dry time when we do not hear or feel God. We are not alone, being disabled, God is right with us

God is our comforter. He really is. "For my yoke is easy, and my burden is light" (Mathew 11:30).

God knows what you ask for before you even ask and the desires of our hearts. It must be in His will. How can He want me to feel bad? I do not think He does. Remember His ways are not ours.

> Take delight in the Lord, He will give you desires
> of your heart. (Psalms 37:4)

What the wicked dread come upon them, but the desire of the righteous will be granted. (Proverbs 10:24)

O Lord, you will hear the desire of the meek; You will strengthen their heart, you will incline Your ear. (Psalm 9:17)

My circumstances just kept on getting bad. The girls and I were playing cards and talking how funny it would be if I were blind. We had a good laugh. We talked about me driving my chair and into things. Well, the following Monday I went blind and went "light blind." It was not everything was dark rather that everything was white and it reminded me of a bad fog; I was not able to see any details. I thought this was bad and I needed to see a doctor. I did not freak out because the girls were always watching, and I had no control over it. I was worried they would feel bad; kids have a way to think somehow anything that happens bad is their fault.

I went to a hospital and saw an eye specialist who told me I was blind due to the pressure in my eyes and the pupil of my eye was not floating but stuck. I had no idea what they were saying. It was all over my head and all I thought was, *I cannot see*. All I heard was the word *blind*. Of course, I bumped into everything and did my makeup by touch. I was proud of being able to do my makeup by touch. I was so surprised—now I am blind too! I went to numerous eye doctor's appointments and had shots right in the eyeball. Good I did not see or I would never let them do that. I had no pain and never knew when they did it. I told my husband not to watch. I felt so blessed to get my eyesight back. God got an earful but I was glad He could handle it. I had problems with my eyes for three months. I say long enough. I do not know how the blind live. It must be hard.

I rely and depend on God. He is like taking a breath. Our God is our God today, right now with a disability. Right as you wait for a breakthrough. We may not be healed till heaven. Choose to follow God as is, now. Do not wait until all is the way you want. Life is not easy.

To me, there is just no way I would be able to exist, I should have been dead. I like the Bible because it tells me where to go, guidelines for my life, and how to act.

> Your word is a lamp to my feet and a light no my path. (Psalms 119:105)

> I can do all things through Him (God) who strengthens me. (Philippians 4:13)

It says, "in all things." You can care for someone or you have a disability and God will take care of all things. That does not mean you will have no problems; hard lesson to learn. I used to seek attention, now I think I get too much attention. I now want to fade in the background but not able to. My chair makes noise and I have a speech impediment; I am kind of noticeable.

I try not to deal with the supernatural. I used to like the shows that went to a place to debunk ghosts like *Ghost Hunters*. I would get so freaked out I would make Tim stay with me to watch them and would not allow the girls to ever watch. In 2008, I lost many important people in my life and this was the year my dad died. I even forgot to tell my in-laws! I really forgot! I remember worrying if my mom was okay. Tim and I took my mom to make some arrangements. I made Tim sleep out in the living room with me because I was worried relatives that died would visit me. How funny! I told you, those shows get to me! I believed the relatives would not go in the living room! Gosh! I have no idea why. Why did I ever do this to myself? I do not watch them now because of the way I would feel.

Long-suffering is a fruit of the Spirit, you do not have to have a disability for the fruit of the Spirit (jot that down). It could come with the loss of a loved one, loss of a job, sickness, illness, you can fill in the blank. It is times like this (hard times); you should stand firm and do not give up. Sometimes we have an angel saying something on one shoulder and a devil on the other (or his thug demons) like in cartoons. The lie will say, "Your situation will never change, you have a disability, look at you!"

The angel says, "It is a lie, stand firm and do not give up." At times like this, you must believe in the Word of God. Do not give up, others with having a disability end up giving up. God is aware of what is happening, He is all-knowing, right? I believe God knows who will listen to Him. I am not special; I am just chicken of the judgement of God. Make a timeline of your life and where God has worked, you will notice God hears your prayers and He has been working hard on your life. Hard to think of when you live with a permanent disability. God sees all our suffering. God is watching over us.

If you told me my disability makes it impossible to laugh, I really could not imagine. If you told me, in my lifetime, so many celebrities were dead, like Robin Williams, I would find it hard to imagine. We never think of us having a disability or taking care of a loved one with a disability. We do not say, "I cannot wait to grow up so I can have a disability." My life has been good and will be in the future. I will not be found rebuking the devil all the time. I will let God think about him and worry about him. Doesn't he take forms?

There was a time, I went on a women's retreat and a lady there never had Chinse food ever. I just could not get over this fact. We had lunch at a Chinese buffet, and I made her go first in line. I made her, I am sure she wanted me to shut up and go away. Then I was so hooked on the fact she never ate Chinse before; I think she liked it. She was protecting her kids from me when she and they were near me. I think she was Amish or Mennonite. I am sure she was afraid I would take forms! I wore too much makeup and was loud.

I have been reading the book of Tobit, that Tobit was blind, disabled like us. You know what healed him? Fish! Gross, but we are desperate to get healed. I would probably bathe in it if I could. I will add the scripture here:

> Then the angel said to him, "Cut open the fish and take out its gall, heart, and liver. Keep them with you but throw away the intestines. For its gall, heart, and liver are useful as medicine." So after cutting open the fish the young man gath-

ered together the gall, heart, and liver; then he
roasted and ate some of the fish and kept some to
be salted. (Tobit 6:5–6)

The demon (thugs are what I call demons) that plagued Tobit's
daughter-in-law, Sarah, the demon who killed all her previous hus-
bands, would go away with the fish parts on incense. That is all it
takes? Interesting to me. Here is the scripture.

> Then Tobias remembered the words of Raphael,
> and he took the fish's liver and heart out of the
> bag where he had them and put them on the
> embers of the incense. The odor of the fish so
> repelled the demon that he fled to the remotest
> parts of Egypt. But Raphael followed him, and
> at once bound him there, hand and foot. I think
> the smell of fish would smell bad. (Tobit 8:3–5)

God's grace is a free unearned gift to us, and we all sin, even
those of us with a disability. The scripture 2 Corinthians 12:9 says,
"But he said to me, 'My grace is sufficient for you, for power is made
perfect in weakness.' So, I will boast all the more gladly of my weak-
nesses, so that the power of Christ may dwell in me.'"

I wrote about this before. You know Paul asked God to take his
problem with his body away. I bet he prayed many times like us. Did
he receive what he asked? Nope, God knew what Paul's future was
and could see around corners. What if God's grace is sufficient for us?
It could be possible, darn it! I want so much to be different; it could
be possible and some people who are disabled never thought about
this. They pray to be healed, which is not a bad thing, and some
people do and some don't.

CHAPTER 4

When I was disabled, I found it hard to handle. My doctors found it hard to believe, my surgeon did not take the stiches out and did not call to check on me. They took out my stiches and it did not hurt a bit. My doctors at the hospital, near my house, told me I had to go to a rehabilitation center. I was thinking of Tim and the girls and wanted to be close to them. I went to Detroit Rehabilitation Center. I had no idea what to expect. I had a hard time to deal with it all. My body just would not obey me and my hands were curled from being paralyzed and I was unable to do a thing about it; I could not even feed myself.

I had a speaker at the top of my head that took all hospital calls. It drove me and my visitors nuts! Boy, I hated that thing! Not an understatement. There I was, living away from Tim and the girls. Everyone was making choices for me. I had a meeting about my care and I sat there, crying, thinking, *This is my life.* I did not say a word. That is not like me; I have plenty to say. I just silently cried.

There was a guy who handled all my disability paperwork. I cried, and he saw me crying and told me he would do all the paperwork. I could not even get a word out. I remember a time Tim and the girls came to visit me, and I held them and could not even speak. I just cried. I was not a crier often; when others cried, I always wished I could cry when others did. I believe this helped me when I counsel others. My husband and kids were all so sweet, and all I could do was hold them. I think I felt bad for everything they had to deal with. I wish none of this happened. I just held them and cried.

Every time I did any activity, my blood would drop and I would pass out. I found it hard to believe because I had no memory of it. One time, they tried to put me in the shower and I passed out on them. The worst was them trying to make me go potty. I felt this was so degrading; you must do it and do not get a choice. See, you would never be in the shower or go potty with anyone. With disability comes others trying to help, but your privacy is always violated. I am a do-it gal.

Tim got so frustrated with students putting my catheter in the wrong place, he learned the right way to do it and we would not let them do it. I would wake up early, a nurse would come in and give me medicine and I would cry upon waking. My nurse would wonder what would make me cry just by waking up! I told her I lost my routine; she wondered what that was. I used to wake up with Tim at 5:00 a.m. and have coffee, watch the news, and hold the girls. I loved my routine. It was gone, I felt what I loss. I felt gibed. Completely gibed. She was so nice and gave me an angel as a gift. She felt bad for me.

I was one who did not cry much to a person who did. I, for a long time, was unable to watch my vacation video or hear our family song, "I'm Yours," without crying or getting upset. I was failing at the rehabilitation center and tried hard to not be sad. I was told that the center insurance said I was not able to stay and I would have to go to a nursing home. It was then I learned I would never walk again, I was devastated. I always thought my neck would be unswollen and then I would walk. At that time, I was thinking I would get better.

There was a time when I was driven in an ambulance to a doctor's appointment. The guys who drove the ambulance did not want to leave me alone with the doctor because Tim was out of the room. I got some shots in my back, and the doctor showed me an X-ray of my spine and said all the swelling was done, and I was shocked. I thought I would walk when the swelling in my spinal cord was done. I was not able to get a word out and cried. The ambulance guys felt bad for me. I let God know how I was feeling. That was the day where I was determined to be the best person in a chair I could be. Me, I thought, I was only thirty-eight years old. The youngest at the nursing home.

So I tried to make the best of it. I spent so long in the nursing home; I could rest. I swore my hands uncurled from the electrodes put on them. I had OT an PT. The therapists seemed to be always in a good mood. I wanted to be left alone. They liked to play games and toss the ball to me. I said, nicely, to give me a deck of cards and leave alone to play solitaire, they seemed thrilled. I was so lucky to get a private room and a television. I got plug-ins and used my faithful cotton candy spray. I am so glad my dad did not see me like this. I bet it was hard for my mom. My dad had dementia and stroke. One time, when he was in a nursing home, he put all his kids' pictures on his lap to leave. I remember seeing him before he died and would bring him coffee and cookies. We would play cards, and he would be so happy he could play rummy and he would win. I saw him after work every other day. At the nursing home I was in, I would go to Meijer Thrifty Acers with those at the home. A guy at the nursing home always bought liquor at the store. He would ride a bus with us and say to girls, "You come at 3:00 p.m. tomorrow," and told me to come over and drink with him at 3:30 p.m. He was hysterical! He gave me joy.

Do you know it is possible to be happy with having a disability? It is real. I think the focus is to be on what we *can* do and not on what we *can't do*. I have bad dark days where I let God know. I unfortunately I get infection many times. I sometimes go to the hospital for high temperatures. I have been septic five times; who ever says that? I had three infections since we moved to Oscoda, Michigan, and was touched in the hospital. I do not like to be touched. At the hospital, I was poked so many times to get a useable vein I have to go through hours and minutes to make it.

Your self-talk is important. What is your inner dialogue? I say don't give the devil ammunition. If you have a dialogue that only focuses on the way you were before, you may feel sad. Yesterday Hope went to the emergency room because of a cyst on her ovary. Tim took her; I wanted to be with her, this is my girl. As the mom, I should be there. Having disabilities, like me, causes me to not be able to go. I had just woken up, and I just am not able to get up and go because my blood pressure drops and all the attention was to be one our youngest. Tim would be worried about her and me. I could have been bent out of shape about it. I had to make a choice not to be upset to not be with her. Do not misunderstand, I was upset and wanted to be with her. Having disabilities, you are forced to make adjustments. I was going to baby her when she got back and all I could pray for her. Having a disability makes you pray a ton. It is really how I survive.

Yesterday Tim and I visited a lighthouse near where we lived. I saw the beach but did not get to lay out as I saw others do. Self-pity came on me and I recognized it, and Tim saw I was so focused on not letting self-pity come, he asked me several times what the matter was. I recognized it and told Tim and had to go minute to minute to not let self-pity have any control; it could. I was so mad, I had to fight self-pity.

I am not a public speaker or writer at all. I am in good company.

But Moses said to the Lord, "O my Lord, I have never been eloquent, neither in the past nor even now that You have spoken to Your servant; but I am slow of speech and slow of tongue." Then the Lord said to him, "Who gives speech to the mortals? Who makes them mute or deaf or seeing or blind? Is it not I, the Lord? Now go, and I will be with your mouth and teach you what you are to speak." But he (Moses) said, "O my Lord, please send someone else." Then the anger of the Lord was kindled against Moses and He said, "What of your brother Aaron, the Levite? I know that he can speak fluently; even now he is coming out to meet you, and when he sees you his heart will be glad. You shall speak to him and put the words in his mouth; and I will be with our mouth and with his mouth and will teach you what you what to do. He indeed shall speak for you to the people; he shall serve as a mouth for you, and you shall serve a God for him." Take in your hand a staff, with which you shall preform the signs." (Exodus 4:10–17)

Now this scripture says, "Anger of the Lord was kindled against Moses," and the Lord says, "Who makes them mute or deaf, seeing or blind? Is it not I, the Lord?" You can say, "Why does God cause deafness or blindness?" I had to look twice at it. The scripture points out a time where God will use disability for His glory. It is true! Look at this:

> They brought to the Pharisees the man who had formerly been blind. Now it was a Sabbath day when Jesus made the mud and opened his eyes. Then the Pharisees also began to ask him how he had received his sight. He said to them, "He put mud on my eyes. Then I washed, and now I see." Some of the Pharisees said, "This man is not from God, for he does not observe the Sabbath." But others said, "How can a man who is a sinner perform such signs?" And they were divided. So they said again to the blind man, "What do you say about him? It was your eyes he opened." He said, "He is a prophet."
>
> The Jews did not believe that he had been blind and had received his sight until they called the parents of the man who had received his sight and asked them, "Is this your son, who you say was born blind? How then does he now see?" His parents answered, "We know that this is our son, and that he was born blind; but we do not know how it is that now he sees, nor do we know who opened his eyes. Ask him; he is of age. He will speak for himself." His parents said this because they were afraid of the Jews; for the Jews had already agreed that anyone who confessed Jesus to be the Messiah would be put out of the synagogue. Therefore his parents said, "He is of age; ask him."
>
> So for the second time they called the man who had been blind, and they said to him, "Give glory to God! We know that this man is a sinner." He answered, "I do not know whether he is a sinner. One thing I do know, that though I

was blind, now I see." They said to him, "What did he do to you? How did he open your eyes?" He answered them, "I have told you already, and you would not listen. Why do you want to hear it again? Do you also want to become his disciples?" Then they reviled him, saying, "You are his disciple, but we are disciples of Moses. We know that God has spoken to Moses, but as for this man, we do not know where he comes from." The man answered, "Here is an astonishing thing! You do not know where he comes from, and yet he opened my eyes. We know that God does not listen to sinners, but he does listen to one who worships him and obeys his will. Never since the world began has it been heard that anyone opened the eyes of a person born blind. If this man were not from God, he could do nothing." They answered him, "You were born entirely in sins, and are you trying to teach us?" And they drove him out. (John 9:1–34)

I got the following story off the Internet and the author is not known. Lessons and resources to help us connect God's Word with our everyday lives.

The Teacup Story

There was a couple who used to go to England to shop in the beautiful stores. They both liked antiques and pottery and especially teacups. This was their twenty-fifth wedding anniversary.

One day in this beautiful shop they saw a beautiful cup. They said, "May we see that? We've never seen one quite so beautiful."

As the lady handed it to them, suddenly the cup spoke. "You don't understand," it said.

"I haven't always been a teacup. There was a time when I was red and I was clay. My master took me and rolled me and patted me over and over and I yelled out, 'let me alone,' but he only smiled, 'Not yet.'

"Then I was placed on a spinning wheel," the cup said, "and suddenly I was spun around and around and around. Stop it! I'm getting dizzy! I screamed. But the master only nodded and said, 'Not yet.'

"Then he put me in the oven. I never felt such heat!" the teacup said. "I wondered why he wanted to burn me, and I yelled and knocked at the door. I could see him through the opening and I could read his lips as He shook his head, 'Not yet.'

"Finally the door opened, he put me on the shelf, and I began to cool. 'There, that's better,' I said. And he brushed and painted me all over. The fumes were horrible. I thought I would gag. 'Stop it, stop it!' I cried. He only nodded, 'Not yet.'

"Then suddenly he put me back into the oven, not like the first one. This was twice as hot and I knew I would suffocate. I begged. I pleaded. I screamed. I cried. All the time I could see him through the opening, nodding his head saying, 'Not yet.'

"Then I knew there wasn't any hope. I would never make it. I was ready to give up. But the door opened and he took me out and placed me on the shelf.

One hour later he handed me a mirror and said, 'Look at yourself.' And I did. I said, 'That's not me; that couldn't be me. It's beautiful. I'm beautiful.'

"'I want you to remember, then,' he said, 'I know it hurts to be rolled and patted, but if I had left you alone, you'd have dried up.

I know it made you dizzy to spin around on the wheel, but if I had stopped, you would have crumbled.

I knew it hurt and was hot and disagreeable in the oven, but if I hadn't put you there, you would have cracked.

I know the fumes were bad when I brushed and painted you all over, but if I hadn't done that, you never would have hardened; you would not have had any color in your life.

And if I hadn't put you back in that second oven, you wouldn't survive for very long because the hardness would not have held.

Now you are a finished product. You are what I had in mind when I first began with you.'"

Following God and letting him be the potter in our lives can be hard and uncomfortable. The way we live our lives matters. "Now, O Lord, you are our Father, we are the clay, and You our potter; And all of us are the work of Your hand" (Isaiah 64:8).

Don't you have times and dark days with having a disability? Sometimes we may feel like a burden and a problem to others. We will not have to deal with it forever. Isn't God coming back? For now, we have to live one day at a time and days turn into weeks, weeks to months, and months to year. We, right now, do not get a choice.

We can forget God's mighty power. It is not our place to ask Him why. It really is none of our business. It is not easy, but we should trust God. Remember, His ways are not our ways. In this life on earth, we will all have something to feel like we are suffering. I look at Job and St. Paul. They had it so bad and felt suffering. No one wants to suffer. We have all these false ways of thinking that we will not suffer being a Christian. Others say, "We're the child of God." You will suffer even more, being a child of God.

Beloved, do not be surprised at the fiery ordeal that is taking place among you to test you, as though something strange were happening to you. But rejoice insofar as you are sharing Christ's sufferings, so that you may also be glad and shout for joy when his glory is revealed. If you are reviled for the name of Christ, you are blessed, because the spirit of glory, which is the Spirit of God, is resting on you. But let none of you suffer as a murderer, a thief, a criminal, or even as a mischief maker. Yet if any of you suffers as a Christian, do not consider it a disgrace, but glorify God because you bear this name. For the time has come for judgment to begin with the household of God; if it begins with us, what will be the end for those who do not obey the gospel of God? And "If it is hard for the righteous to be save what will become of the ungodly and the sinners?" Therefore, let those suffering in accordance with God's will entrust themselves to a faithful Creator, while continuing to do good. (1 Peter 4:12-19)

Of course, God wants us to feel good! When I got diagnosed, my dreams were loss-of-control dreams. I like having control and did not have a say now I was paralyzed. My physical therapy goal at the hospital was to sit up. I was lucky this was in my dreams only because I can get so mad. I knew I would get my healing in heaven or on this earth. I would have to be sedated if I got it on earth. I was faced with what I do in the waiting time of getting healing. I learned. I am not normally a patient person; you learn to be patient with a disability or you will be miserable. Others have some control over you, and you make tons of mistakes with your body like dropping stuff. You may feel like our mountains are unmovable. We may have to wait for heaven for new working bodies. Stinks, doesn't it? It is our life and those close to us. We all are forced to change and do things differently.

Waiting is not an easy thing to do; we must wait. What do you do with the waiting?

> Therefore beloved, while you are waiting for these things, strive to be found by Him in peace, without a spot or blemish, and regard the patience of our Lord as salvation. So also, our beloved brother Paul wrote you according to the wisdom given to him, speaking of this as he does in all his letters. There are some things in them hard to understand, which the ignorant and unstable twist to their own destruction, as they do the other scriptures. You, therefore, beloved, since for you were forewarned, beware that you are not carried away with the error of the lawless and your own stability. But grow in the grace and knowledge of our Lord and Savior Jesus Christ. To Him be the glory both now and to the day of eternity. (2 Peter 3:14–18)

Spotless or without blemish! Patient! Not anything like me, naturally. How can I be like this? Did you know we all have all we need to live a Christian life? I know it is hard to believe.

> His divine power has given us everything needed for life and Godliness., through the knowledge of Him who called by His own glory and goodness. Thus, He has given us, through these things, His precious and very great promises, so that them you may escape from the corruption that is in the world, because of lust, and may become participants of the divine nature. (2 Peter 1:3–11)

After the stroke, I was weak in the arms, I cannot even write. I had to learn to breathe and eat again, so many ways I had to relearn. You are in a place of waiting. To be honest, I hate to wait. Waiting and being still is hard for me. I know God is working, but I still want to go before Him to make things happen. I have a time line and want God to act faster. I have to practice this a lot. In the following scriptures, the Israelites were about to cross the Red Sea and was told and be still for God as he works.

> But Moses said to the people, "Do not be afraid, stand firm, and see the deliverance that the Lord will accomplish for you today; for the Egyptians whom you see today you shall never see again. The Lord will fight for you, and you have only to keep still." (Exodus 14:13–14)

> Do not worry about anything, but in everything by prayer and supplication with thanksgiving let your requests be made known to God. And the peace of God, which surpasses all understanding, will guard your hearts and your minds in Christ Jesus. (Philippians 4:6–7)

We all have hard times. These days we have fidgets and stress balls to handle stress. It seems everyone has anxiety or a disability. We all have some stress at times. My oldest makes stress balls and gave me one. Good OT by the way. She makes some out of balloons and rice and some with flour. Tim got a flour one and I warned him to be careful not to break it. He was driving and it broke, and flour went all over him. What a mess, *stress*! I could see it happening in slow motion. We both laughed, and I think rice ones are better.

If I have a beginning or the first inkling of a problem, I must pray to God. Things can be too big for me to handle alone. I pray a lot. I say it over and over again, "If you have problems, it is better not to deal with them alone. Why not have God on our side?" What ever happened to laying our care on him?

I watched *Dr. Strange* with the family because we have never seen it. I prayed during that movie because I related to Dr. Strange losing his hands, being disabled was a part of my life. I did all to prevent myself from crying. It bothered me the rest of the time after the movie. I thought he played devastation and angry about all changing good. With a disability, your life changes fast; it is different.

Crisis comes as a loss of a child, loss of a job, a bad illness or even death. You might say, "How can this be? I am child of God." I look at St. Paul's life and think he had it mostly bad. He seemed to have bad circumstances.

He was a child of God too. He got flogged, and you know that had to hurt. I think when he was getting flogged, he thought he could use a miracle right then. He did not get a miracle right then. He was still left for dead, one time. How could anything bad in our lives be fine with God? I do not buy this life is going to be perfect.

"The Lord sustains them on their sick bed; in their illness, you heal all their infirmities" (Psalms 41:3). You may get healing here on earth or in heaven. You will be healed. I would love it now on earth and not in heaven; I am a poor person to wait.

Out of curiosity, do people look at you? I would look before my injury too. I would go to the girls' school functions and saw others look and stare at me. I felt embarrassed and like a circus animal. They were just being curious.

We expect a breakthrough. We all, at times, think we will be happier when; when may not come. I used to pray, "Lord I will be happy when I am healed." I pray now for the Lord to help me deal with not being healed. See the difference? I wish I never was disabled. I was at a store to buy gardening stuff and would look at all the flowers and vegetable stuff. I used to garden and can, now I am unable to do them.

See, if I choose to focus on that, then I would be depressed. I have learned now; I have to always practice thinking of all the stuff I can do. Jonah had it bad, he felt waves and was swallowed by a fish. I would guess that was not pleasant. You can still have the bad times and a *breakthrough* may never come. This is hard to accept. Does this mean we give up to God? I do not know about you, I need Him. I am an optimist and tell myself the Lord is working. I look back on my life and know the Lord had His hand on my life. This keeps me going at the dry times of my life and at bad times. Jonah had it bad and said the following to God in the belly of the fish. We may have a disability but being in a fish belly has to be bad hard time.

"And thus is the boldness we have in Him, that if we ask anything *according to His will,* He hears us, and if we know that He hears us in whatever we ask, we know that we have obtained the requests made of Him" (1 John 5:14-15). I do not buy into the good life, getting everything I want. Of course, God wants us to feel good. We live in a fallen world, sometimes we make mistakes; others make mistakes, or it is coincidence. I do not look for a devil or angel around every corner. He is in charge. There is not one thing we can do to get healed.

CHAPTER 5

The caregivers struggle too, I never complained to anyone but God because He can deal with it. I did not want to wear out my caregivers, and I was not much of a complainer anyway. You can wear out caregivers. They will not tell you or make it known to you. They will feel so guilty for not having the disability. Listen for tones of the voice and body cues, nonverbals, to help me know. It is very important to not take it personally. It is very important, if you have a disability, to acknowledge their help. They can wear out fast. This is normal. I always think having a disability is hard for *all* involved. It does not just happen to you. It is very wise to know their lives are altered too. I think the worst is turning into yourself. This is so easy to do. I fight this all the time. Do you know that you can make yourself an idol too? Anything you make more important than God can be considered an idol.

If you really think about your life, it could be worst. I have it cushy when you truly think about it. I have fresh water, a bed with covers above ground, food brought to me, and I live in America. I am married to Tim; he has brought me a fresh cup of coffee in the morning always. It could always be worse.

I went to Hope's school's first football game, and I like going out. There was a guy there and a girl in a wheelchair. The little girl had a tracheotomy and could not do much. The guy talked to me and liked the feature of my chair that goes up. We have the chair in common and realized they and their love ones have suffered some. I am an optimist and always think it could be worse. Seeing a girl with a tracheotomy reminded me of being worse. I could have had ended up with one, and my husband would freak out. Prior to the game, Tim and I went shopping due to the fact we live twenty-four miles from where we shopped. We took coolers with us and a lady from the store brought us some ice for them. We were so thankful, we forgot the ice. Appalachia is so different from Detroit. In Detroit, the stores are near and the people seems stay to themselves more.

Grace's husband, Andrew Bolin, told me about a lady from Rwanda, Africa, who escaped the genocide, and lived in a death camp for ten years. I remember feeling so bothered about the genocide in Kosovo, was so upset about the refugees in Syria right now in 2016.

Tim workers as a chaplain at a prison. Now that is bad. It does not get sicker than prisoners. I am lucky to not have a tracheotomy and use of my arms and hands. I might take thirty minutes to put on a watch but at least I can put it on and wear one. I like to clean and cook. I am weird like that. I like to fold laundry for physical therapy. It takes me a long time, and it is painful for others to see. I get it done though.

For occupational therapy, I like to do makeup and puzzles. I am addicted to any games and love playing cards with Tim and friends. Once I tried to use chopsticks like I used to before I had a disability, and it was a disaster. I made a huge mess, but we thought it was funny. It is not easy to eat with chopsticks with no disability. I really think it could be much worse.

If you have a disability, we, at times, learn to use other senses. It is just that way; our bodies may be broken. I do laundry this way, I use my reacher and feel the laundry in the washing machine. I cannot fully see so I feel.

Having a disability means adjustments. I do some things I did before having a disability; I expect shaking and dropping much and do not get upset. The fact is, I am disabled and it takes me longer to cook and do stuff. Yesterday I hated my disability; I have good and bad days. I was cooking and got my chair stuck between the cabinet and the stove. I broke the glass on the stove door. I felt like I was a burden. See, with a disability, I think the one lie that is presented before me, time after time, is you're a burden. It just does not be a one-time thing. Being a burden will be a falsehood that has been before me, time and time again. I am loved by my friends and family. They would not want me to feel this way. They would rather be here with me with a disability than not. I do all I can for myself and then ask for help.

I tried to sweep and then mop. I could not sweep well but was able to mop with no problem. I made Tim and myself pancakes, and it was like the chopstick incident that did not go so well. I have places on my arms that have no feelings, and I burned myself and did not know. I lost my cooking privileges without someone watching. What did I do? I organized the laundry room and told Tim and Hope it is not to ever be messy again. I was careful and put my chair down and on low speed and I made no dents or scratches. The one thing that was hard for me was the ironing board. The darn thing kept on opening, it took at least a long time for me to get it closed and to lean against the wall.

I do try things for myself like cleaning. So I decided to contribute to my family; if you have a disability and are the provider, there is so much we cannot do. I asked Tim if I can boss him around in the kitchen and he lets me. I am a Sicilian girl and the kitchen is my domain. I hate not being able to cook or clean. Tim and the girls would cook and clean, and the way I would do it is differently. It is so hard to see them make my grandmother's S-cookies and I am not able to. See, you are forced to have no control. I think this has been the hardest for me to learn. I would say to myself, "What would I be like today, having a disability?"

Before I was injured, there was a time I was holding my youngest, Hope, Tim was telling me about dog. As soon as he talked about the dog, I heard the words in my head, *It will be okay.* I knew what that meant, I used to be a person who did not like any animals. I told Tim we had to get that dog today no matter what. If you knew me, I was truly not an animal kind of girl. I used to never want to own a dog or cat, etc. I had a fish that would jump out of fish tank. I owned a suicidal fish. Not as relaxing as I hoped.

Okay, back to the dog. I had no idea what kind of dog it was. I had no idea what it even looked like. I got lucky; our small dog, Lilly, was perfect for us and I fell in love. The girls could not believe it. They knew how I used to feel about owning animals and thought we're babysitting the dog. They were so surprised she was ours to keep. The dog was happiness each day. I lived away for a year, and God must have known and provided this for the girls. He has given me joy too; she will jump on my lap today still. I get to hold her. I would love it when my friend would sneak Lilly in the hospital and she would be as excited as me. Tim and I eventually moved up to Michigan from Kentucky. Lilly handled it well. We took her to the veterinarian, and she weighed too much. We put her on a diet, and she lost weight. We took her to the veterinarian in Michigan, and she was underweight and had diabetes. She had to stay in the hospital to have her sugar taken care of. I cried and could not get a word out. I was a girl in a wheelchair, crying at the doctor; they were trying to help me be fine. Crying is one thing but crying and in a wheelchair is seen as bad. I never board her she is my baby, now she had to stay. I had missed her and my arms ached for her. I have to deal with this and knew God would get me through this as He has been there for me at hard times in the past. This would be no different.

I am blessed to have Tim who takes good care of me. He goes beyond because he loves me and sees marriage as a sacrament. I never wanted a disability or all it entails. My family, who was deeply affected by it, did not want one either. If you are a caretaker or have a disability, it changes the whole family. You may have a disability, but it affects those who love us too

Disability does not just happen to you. People will say, "If there was a God, then why all the suffering in this world?" I never understood until I read His ways are not ours. We live in a fallen world where some others do not lead a Christian life.

> If anyone member suffers, all suffer together with it; if one member if one member is honored, all rejoice together with it. (1 Corinthians 12:26)

> And not only that, we can boast our sufferings, knowing that suffering produces endurance and endurance produces character, and character produces hope and hope does not disappoints us, because God's love has been poured into our

hearts through the Holy Spirit that has been given to us. (Romans 5:3–5)

Well, that scripture settles it! I am producing right where I am, with or without a disability.

I pray the rosary daily and think about the Mother Mary next to me, praying on my behalf. I was thinking of the scripture of two or more praying, God is there. Mathew 18:20 says, "For where two or three are gathered in my name, I am there among them." I think to myself, *Mother Mary is agreeing and praying on my behalf when I pray the rosary. She is my plus one, she is equaling two.*

CHAPTER 6

With disability, you will sometimes have no control of your disability. Menopause came early—age forty-two. Lucky me! I am not fifty years old yet! The only symptoms I have are heat flashes and weight gain. There is no denying it; I do not like either one. I can handle the weight gain but the hot flashes are hard to handle when you have disability and without one. We have no control. I tell Tim, "Menopause is kicking my butt!" See, you can have a disability and still get the normal things of life, like menopause; disability does not change that. Can you believe menopause affects Tim who is my caregiver? He knows when I get hot flashes, and then I sweat and get cold. I need to be changed at times. My family are sick of me for being hot and cold. I tell them to adjust the thermostat and will say to turn on the fan but will turn around and tell to turn it off. Life is going on whether you have a disability or not. Life goes on.

I love the Hymn "It Is Well with My Soul." The following, I got from stagustine.com on the Internet.

> Horatio G. Spafford was a successful lawyer and businessman in Chicago with a lovely family—a wife, Anna, and five children. However, they were not strangers to tears and tragedy. Their young son died with pneumonia in 1871, and in that same year, much of their business was lost in the great Chicago fire. Yet, God in His mercy and kindness allowed the business to flourish once more.
>
> On Nov. 21, 1873, the French ocean liner, Ville du Havre was crossing the Atlantic from the

U.S. to Europe with 313 passengers on board. Among the passengers were Mrs. Spafford and their four daughters. Although Mr. Spafford had planned to go with his family, he found it necessary to stay in Chicago to help solve an unexpected business problem. He told his wife he would join her and their children in Europe a few days later. His plan was to take another ship.

About four days into the crossing of the Atlantic, the Ville du Harve collided with a powerful, iron-hulled Scottish ship, the Loch Earn. Suddenly, all of those on board were in grave danger. Anna hurriedly brought her four children to the deck. She knelt there with Annie, Margaret Lee, Bessie and Tanetta and prayed that God would spare them if that could be His will, or to make them willing to endure whatever awaited them. Within approximately 12 minutes, the Ville du Harve slipped beneath the dark waters of the Atlantic, carrying with it 226 of the passengers including the four Spafford children.

A sailor, rowing a small boat over the spot where the ship went down, spotted a woman floating on a piece of the wreckage. It was Anna, still alive. He pulled her into the boat and they were picked up by another large vessel which, nine days later, landed them in Cardiff, Wales. From there she wired her husband a message which began, "Saved alone, what shall I do?" Mr. Spafford later framed the telegram and placed it in his office.

Another of the ship's survivors, Pastor Weiss, later recalled Anna saying, "God gave me four daughters. Now they have been taken from me. Someday I will understand why."

Mr. Spafford booked passage on the next available ship and left to join his grieving wife. With the ship about four days out, the captain called Spafford to his cabin and told him they were over the place where his children went down.

According to Bertha Spafford Vester, a daughter born after the tragedy, Spafford wrote "It Is Well with My Soul" while on this journey.

When peace like a river attendeth my way,
When sorrows like sea billows roll,
Whatever my lot, thou hast taught me to say,
It is well, it is well with my soul.
Chorus:
It is well with my soul,
It is well, it is well with my soul

Anna gave birth to three more children, one of which died at age four with dreaded pneumonia. In August 1881, the Spaffords moved to Jerusalem. Mr. Spafford died and is buried in that city.

Now I have to tell you all something too funny. I call below the line of my injury, C7 to T2, I like to call it the music machine. I have no idea when it goes off; my leg will shake violently, I could break wind or my right leg and foot will fall. Hope, my youngest daughter, and I were at the doctor's office for her checkup (Tim dropped us off). We were in a very small room with a nurse and I broke wind. I was starting to smile and Hope knew what was happening. I told the nurse to please excuse me and she left the room. I started to smile big and told Hope I could not look at her and she laughed. It was too funny! Because I cannot laugh does not mean I do not have a sense of humor. When you have disability, there is plenty to laugh at.

God knows when I freak out and what I freak out about. I am such a city girl, I really am. We visited Michigan and the fish flies (mayflies) were everywhere! Did I freak out? Why, yes, I did. Tim has to get new wipers for the car, there were so many. I even prayed to God about them getting on me. I grew up in St. Clair Shores with them; if you are near a lake, you will know what they are. Businesses have to spray their windows with the hose, and street cleaners come and clean the streets with them to avoid accidents; they are slimy things. When I moved to Michigan from Kentucky and did social work, I made home visits to St. Clair Shores at fish fly time. I forgot what it was like to have fish flies. I would use whatever writing device on hand to ring the doorbell; there was no way I would knock on the door.

I get so excited about living in the Daniel Boone National Forest. I like to sit on my deck and see all the wildlife. We get bears, coyotes, turkeys, and lots of deer. If there is something dangerous like a bear, the prison where Tim is a chaplain will call and tell us. One time, they called and said there were bear cubs in our yard. What? I thought their mom was close by. I like watching the deer; my family gets sick of me trying to say, "My, there is a deer" in my new voice, I was excited. I sound like I have something wrong because I cannot say. Remember, I have a speech impediment. I even dreamt about it in a dream. In all my dreams I had, I can feel, walk, and talk.

I was on a rocky path with God. I told him, "Please change Your mind, I am not handling being with disability well. He had a specific plan to use my disability, is what he said. I wanted the Lord to change His mind. Darn, I was hoping this was not true, and I begged Him to heal me and change His mind. I felt Him using me because I listen and live my life the way He would have wanted. That was all my dream. I told all the bad that happened to me was hard to deal with. We all have long-suffering sometimes. Romans 2:4–8 says:

> Do you despise the riches of his kindness and for-
> bearance and patience? Do you not realize that
> God's kindness is meant to lead you to repen-
> tance? But by your hard and impenitent heart
> you are storing up wrath for yourself on the day
> of wrath, when God's righteous judgment will
> be revealed. For he will repay according to each

one's deeds: to those who by patiently doing good
seek for glory and honor and immortality, he will
give eternal life; while for those who are self-seek-
ing and who obey not the truth but wickedness,
there will be wrath and fury.

I am so impatient and must work on it. Having long-suffering is hard; with a disability, it is harder because things like cooking, cleaning, and even what you wish you look like is not what you
would want. Long-suffering is a fruit of the Spirit; you do not have
to have a disability for the fruit of the Spirit. It could come in the
loss of a loved one, loss of a job, sickness, illness, you can fill in the
blanks. It is times like these (hard times) you should stand firm and
do not give up.

Tim came into our bedroom and then said the unimaginable—
he told me there was a snake under my bed and it was up like it
wanted to strike. Snake! You got to be kidding! Under *my bed*, this
must be a joke. Tim, my husband, said, "Hold still!" The way and
tone of his voice was telling me something bad was under my bed.
He meant business. My dog, Lilly, was growling and barking, her bed
was under my bed too! I held still and even held my breath. I froze.
It was like a skunk was walking by me, I wanted to run. I thought it
was a big spider—snake or spider? Both would freak me out and I do
not care for. I did not get to flee because of not being able to move. I
wanted to flee, it was me or the snake. I was so lucky it was not in my
bed with me; I was ready to roll out of bed if I had to. This incident
scared me, it was a rat snake which are fast; I felt violated. Whoever
says they have ever had a snake under their bed? Me! I have a fun
story to tell. It was not funny when it happened, but it is funny now.
I have been held hostage by spiders before and survived; this will be
no different. With disabilities comes adjustments.

As Christians, we need to live in the moment. Yesterday has
happened, and the future has not happened yet. We all are going
to die sometime. We all have the same fate as everyone else, in spite
of if we were the prettiest, smartest, richest, and funniest person. I
was talking earlier about living in the moment. I was going to see

my cousin and friends from high school, and I had to put into practice living in the moment. I was not going to think about being the smartest, prettiest, and funniest person in the room. I ended up forgetting all about it, we and had fun. We talked and laughed at a time a girl we did not know was threatening to beat her up because my friend would unplug the video game she was playing before she was about to win. The girl who was threatening my friend put her finger on my friend's nose and smashed it. This made us laugh hard, and she left. I felt free in a way, not the prettiest, smartest, or the funniest in the room. We need to remember, we will all stand before the Lord.

Romans 14:4 explains it well, "Who are you to pass judgment on servants of another? It is before their own lord that they stand or fall. And they will be upheld, for the Lord is able to make them stand." I have to be honest, I do judge. I was shopping at Walmart, and in the checkout line with Tim, a guy rested his foot on my chair. I could feel the pressure, my chair would tilt up and down. I couldn't believe this was happening. I thought he was going to try to steal my purse. If he was, I would run him over and cause a huge scene. Others can see me as an easy target. Tim saw him get too close. Tim is protective of me, and he was going to say he was too close, and we checked out. Tim did not know he did that to my chair or Tim would have let him have it. Two days later, we were at Mass and a lady used the arm of my chair at communion to rise up. Tim and I saw it and we lost it. We laughed and thought it was funny. Right the in Mass, we lost it. Now at Walmart was funny and rude; when it happened at Mass, it was hilarious. I guess when you have a disability, others think they get you and have no boundaries for personal space.

The Lord knows we feel at the hard times. I got to go to Liberty Kentucky and attend The Society of Saint John Missionaries. It was packed with people and I was treated well. Those of us who have a disability know others find it hard to deal with us; it is not their fault, hard. It is just something that goes with a disability. I was sitting alone and working hard to stay out of the way. I have taken others out by mistake and did not want to hurt anyone. When I was sitting alone, I saw an elderly guy sitting alone and I wanted to talk with him. He gave me a look that said he knew how it feels being alone.

See, I am an extrovert naturally, but I have several disabilities and a speech problem. He would have really had a hard time listening to me. I bet he felt bad and found it hard to be elderly. I lived in a nursing home for months when I was paralyzed and really got a taste of what it means to be elderly. I am sure this man that I saw was different when he was young. It is how we feel when we vision ourselves before any disability.

It was about to be Lent and I was living in a nursing home. I was going to give up something. It was the least I could do. Lent for me is always where I got better spiritually. It was then I stopped living by my feelings; this was hard. So I prayed to God, what I was going to give up was my feelings. This meant I would give Him every feeling I had. I decided I would not live anymore on my feelings and just on His Word. My feelings were all bad, and I felt hopeless; I was so sad. If a bad thought would enter my mind—there were many—I would see if it was not biblical, I would toss it out if a thought was not in line with the Bible. I was all over the place and was not sure if I was hearing form God or not.

God's Word is what you have to rely on when you're disabled. Here are some verses that are used to rely on God's Word.

> Your word is a lamp to my feet and a light to my
> path, I held this close when I was not disabled.
> (Psalms 119:105)

> The grass withers, the flower fades; but the word
> of our God will stand forever. (Isaiah 40:8)

I do not know about you but these verses help. Now back to scriptures on God's Word.

> Heaven and earth will pass away, but my words
> will not pass away. (Matthew 25:35)

> In the beginning was the Word, and the Word was
> with God, and the Word was God. (John 1:1)

And the Word became flesh and lived among us,
and we have seen his glory, the glory as of a father's
only son, full of grace and truth. (John 1:14)

Even some of God's words are letter and stories, we can still rely on them. I can read some of them and they are never old and I learn a new lesson. Come on I can't be the only one?

It is the spirit that gives life; the flesh is useless.
The words that I have spoken to you are spirit
and life. (Matthew 6:63)

The one who rejects me and does not receive my
word has a judge; on the last day the word that
I have spoken will serve as judge, for I have not
spoken on my own, but the Father who sent me
has himself given me a commandment about
what to say and what to speak. And I know that
his commandment is eternal life. What I speak,
therefore, I speak just as the Father has told me."
(John 12:48–50)

Better listen to God. Word of God is important; it must be. The Word is part of the armor of God.

Finally, be strong in the Lord and in the strength
of his power. Put on the whole armor of God, so
that you may be able to stand against the wiles of
the devil. For our struggle is not against enemies of
blood and flesh, but against the rulers, against the
authorities, against the cosmic powers of this present darkness, against the spiritual forces of evil in
the heavenly places. Therefore take up the whole
armor of God, so that you may be able to with-
stand on that evil day, and having done everything,
to stand firm. Stand therefore, and fasten the belt

of truth around your waist, and put on the breast-plate of righteousness. As shoes for your feet put on whatever will make you ready to proclaim the gospel of peace. With all of these take the shield of faith, with which you will be able to quench all the flaming arrows of the evil one. Take the helmet of salvation, and the sword of the Spirit, which is the word of. (Ephesians 6:10–17)

See? While we are parked here, the benefits of having the sword of the Spirit. It is perfection for us; finally, be strong in the Lord and in the strength of his power.

Put on the whole armor of God, so that you may be able to stand against the wiles of the devil. For our struggle is not against enemies of blood and flesh, but against the rulers, against the author-ities, against the cosmic powers of this present darkness, against the spiritual forces of evil in the heavenly places. Therefore take up the whole armor of God, so that you may be able to with-stand on that evil day, and having done every-thing, to stand firm.

I do not want to know the principalities of darkness. I will take the strength and protection to ward off the devil. The *Free Dictionary* online defines *armor* as the following:

- Noun: the metal coverings formerly worn by soldiers or warriors to protect the body in battle. "Knights in armor"
- Verb: provide (someone) with emotional, social, or other defenses. "The knowledge armored him against her"

I have a peace that surpasses understanding. I am disabled, and all our stuff seems to break like a van for my chair. I am surprised I am so calm and not worrying. There is nothing we can do to fix it, not one thing. I know, from the past, God is working for my good.

Also when I had a negative thought, I would thank God for loving me perfectly and knowing what I wanted or needed. I was desperate and felt the enemy could make you think a thought was from God. He is so tricky and we can be duped so easily. I remember a psychologist came and saw me and said I was depressed. I said, "Of course I was, situational depression."

I was the one who would play jokes on psychologists. One time, I put a fart machine in the psychologist's pocket! Funny to me. Anyways, I knew God's Word was true and my circumstances seemed bad. I was thirty eight years old in a nursing home, not being able to move. One time, I got myself tangled in the bed control, blower, and straightener. A nurse came in to give me medicine and asked me what I was doing. I looked at her and was caught; she was afraid I would burn myself.

Every Thursday, my cousin Christina would come and bring Chinese food and watch *Grey's Anatomy* with me. This was fun, I looked forward to it. I am sure there were times she did not feel like coming but did. As a caregiver, we rely so heavy on them and feel like a burden too. Caregivers do what they do not feel like doing like helping; it can be gross, C-Diff, or being changed. Really, if you do not set out to be a caregiver and it is not part of job, it is normal to hate it. At this time, I was reminded that I cannot be responsible for the happiness for others; *you and I cannot be responsible for others' happiness.* The happiness of others is too big for us and can be prideful at times, like we can have any control over anyone. Really, are you God?

The disciples had not a bit of control. Can you imagine how the disciples were feeling after Jesus was crucified, dead, and buried? Hiding and fearful of the Jews, after they saw their Lord crucified. They were on high alert. They saw what happened to Jesus. I get tickled with the following scripture:

> When it was evening on that day, the first day
> of the week, and the doors of the house where
> the disciples had met were locked for fear of the

Jews, Jesus came and stood among them and said, "Peace be with you." After he said this, he showed them his hands and his side. Then the disciples rejoiced when they saw the Lord. Jesus said to them again, "Peace be with you. As the Father has sent me, so I send you." When he had said this, he breathed on them and said to them, "Receive the Holy Spirit. If you forgive the sins of any, they have forgiven them; if you retain the sins of any, they are retained." (John 20:19–23)

Can you imagine sitting there and minding their own business and Jesus appeared to them? Remember, Jesus had to say, "Peace be with you," twice. Come on, can you imagine? I like to think He said that twice because He knew seeing Him appear would freak them out.

We who have a disability have to trust God in everything. If we were meant, this second, to have what we want—healing—He must know what we want and could make it so and give what we want. It a different kind of trust called, especially with a disability. God knows what is best.

I got the following story on the Internet.

Pearl Story: The Pearl Necklace

The cheerful girl with bouncy golden curls was almost five. Waiting with her mother at the checkout stand, she saw them: a circle of glistening white pearls in a pink foil box.

"Oh please, Mommy. Can I have them? Please, Mommy, please!"

Quickly the mother checked the back of the little foil box and then looked back into the pleading blue eyes of her little girl's upturned face.

"A dollar ninety-five. That's almost $2.00. If you really want them, I'll think of some extra chores for you and in no time you can save enough money to buy them for yourself. Your birthday's only a week away and you might get another crisp dollar bill from Grandma."

As soon as Jenny got home, she emptied her penny bank and counted out 17 pennies. After dinner, she did more than her share of chores and she went to the neighbor and asked Mrs. McJames if she could pick dandelions for ten cents.

On her birthday, Grandma did give her another new dollar bill and at last she had enough money to buy the necklace.

Jenny loved her pearls. They made her feel dressed up and grown up. She wore them every-where—Sunday school, kindergarten, even to bed. The only time she took them off was when she went swimming or had a bubble bath. Mother said if they got wet, they might turn her neck green.

Jenny had a very loving daddy and every night when she was ready for bed, he would stop whatever he was doing and come upstairs to read her a story. One night when he finished the story, he asked Jenny, "Do you love me?"

"Oh yes, Daddy. You know that I love you."

"Then give me your pearls."

"Oh, Daddy, not my pearls. But you can have Princess—the white horse from my collection. The one with the pink tail. Remember, Daddy? The one you gave me. She's my favorite."

"That's okay, Honey. Daddy loves you. Good night." And he brushed her cheek with a kiss.

About a week later, after the story time, Jenny's daddy asked again, "Do you love me?"

"Daddy, you know I love you."

"Then give me your pearls."

"Oh Daddy, not my pearls. But you can have my baby doll. The brand new one I got for my birthday. She is so beautiful, and you can have the yellow blanket that matches her sleeper."

"That's okay. Sleep well. God bless you, little one. Daddy loves you." And as always, he brushed her cheek with a gentle kiss.

A few nights later when her daddy came in, Jenny was sitting on her bed with her legs crossed Indian-style. As he came close, he noticed her chin was trembling and one silent tear rolled down her cheek.

"What is it, Jenny? What's the matter?"

Jenny didn't say anything but lifted her little hand up to her daddy. And when she opened it, there was her little pearl necklace. With a little quiver, she finally said, "Here, Daddy. It's for you."

With tears gathering in his own eyes, Jenny's kind daddy reached out with one hand to take the dime-store necklace, and with the other hand he reached into his pocket and pulled out a blue velvet case with a strand of genuine pearls and gave them to Jenny.

He had them all the time. He was just waiting for her to give up the dime-store stuff so he could give her genuine treasure.

What are you hanging on to? Not having a broken body, God wants us to enjoy life right now. You may say how? With a broken body, enjoy the journey of this life. "The thief comes only to steal and kill and destroy. I came that they may have life and have it abundantly" (John 10:10).

Do you know that Mother Teresa left her journals here and felt she was not loved by God? I was told to me by Tim this. He is like a walking encyclopedia. My girls are the same way, they read a lot. I got this about her from Biographies Online.

> Mother Teresa was born in 1910 in Skopje, capital of the Republic of Macedonia. Little is known about her early life, but at a young age she felt a calling to be a nun and serve through helping the poor. At the age of 18 she was given permission to join a group of nuns in Ireland. After a few months of training, with the Sisters of Loreto, she was then given permission to travel to India. She took her formal religious vows in 1931 and chose to be named after St Therese of Lisieux—the patron saint of missionaries.
>
> On her arrival in India, she began by working as a teacher, however the widespread poverty of Calcutta made a deep impression on her and this led to her starting a new order called "The Missionaries of Charity". The primary objective of this mission was to look after people, who nobody else was prepared to look after. Mother Teresa felt that serving others was a key principle of the teachings of Jesus Christ. She often mentioned the saying of Jesus, "Whatever you do to the least of my brethren, you do it to me."
>
> As Mother Teresa said herself: "Love cannot remain by itself—it has no meaning. Love has to be put into action, and that action is service."—Mother Teresa
>
> She experienced two particularly traumatic periods in Calcutta. The first was the Bengal famine of 1943 and the second was the Hindu/Muslim violence in 1946, before the partition of India. In 1948, she left the convent to live full-time among the poorest of Calcutta. She chose to wear a white Indian sari, with a blue border,

out of respect for the traditional Indian dress. For many years, Mother Teresa and a small band of fellow nuns survived on minimal income and food, often having to beg for funds. But, slowly her efforts with the poorest were noted and appreciated by the local community and Indian politicians.

In 1952, she opened her first home for the dying, which allowed people to die with dignity. Mother Teresa often spent time with those who were dying. Some have criticized the lack of proper medical attention, and their refusal to give painkillers. Others say that it afforded many neglected people the opportunity to die knowing that someone cared. Over time the work grew. Missions were started overseas, and by 2013, there are 700 missions operating in over 130 countries. The scope of their work also expanded to include orphanages, and hospices for those with terminal illness. "Not all of us can do great things. But we can do small things with great love."—Mother Teresa

Mother Teresa never sought to convert those of another faith. Those in her hospices were given the religious rites appropriate to their faith. However, she had a very firm Catholic faith and took a strict line on abortion, the death penalty and divorce—even if her position was unpopular. Her whole life was influenced by her faith and religion, even though at times she confessed she didn't feel the presence of God.

The Missionaries of Charity now has branches throughout the world including branches in the developed world where they work with the homeless and people affected with AIDS. In 1965, the organization became an International Religious Family by a decree of Pope Paul VI.

In the 1960s, the life of Mother Teresa was first brought to a wider public attention by Malcolm Muggeridge who wrote a book and produced a documentary called "Something Beautiful for God".

In 1979, she was awarded the Nobel Peace Prize "for work undertaken in the struggle to overcome poverty and distress, which also constitutes a threat to peace." She didn't attend the ceremonial banquet but asked that the $192,000 fund be given to the poor. In later years, she was more active in western developed countries. She commented that though the West was materially prosperous, there was often a spiritual poverty. "The hunger for love is much more difficult to remove than the hunger for bread." When she was asked how to promote world peace, she replied, "Go home and love your family".

Over the last two decades of her life, Mother Teresa suffered various health problems, but nothing could dissuade her from fulfilling her mission of serving the poor and needy. Until her very last illness she was active in travelling around the world to the different branches of The Missionaries of Charity. During her last few years, she met Princess Diana in the Bronx, New York. The two died within a week of each other. Following Mother Teresa's death, the Vatican began the process of beatification, which is the second step on the way to canonization and sainthood. Mother Teresa was formally beatified in October 2003 by Pope John Paul II. In September 2015, Pope Francis declared: "Mother Teresa, in all aspects of her life, was a generous dispenser of divine mercy, making herself available for everyone through her welcome and defense of human life, those unborn and those abandoned and discarded, "She bowed down before those who were spent, left to die on the side of the road, seeing in them their God-given dignity. She made her voice heard before the powers of this world, so that they might recognize their guilt for the crime of poverty they created. Mother Teresa was a living saint who offered a great example and inspiration to the world."

I am glad they made her a saint. I bet she was so surprised to find out she was loved by God and named a saint! I was thinking, *If she felt that way, we all are domed.* I get how she felt; don't you feel the same way with a disability or being a caregiver? Last night, I turned off my television at three thirty. I do not normally have trouble sleeping right now; I did when I was first injured. This night, I did. I had what I call a spiritual fit. I got angry and so mad at God and it affected my sleeping. I told God I was sick of all my hard times and felt life was not fair. I told Him that His Word did not match up to my life. Why do others, especially celebrities, seem to have all? I told Him the some do not even follow His commandments. I told Him, I was stuck in this world and couldn't He toss me a bone! I fought with Him most of the night.

In the morning, I said sorry and knew there had to be something I was missing. I must have, it is okay to not know everything. I bet we do not know stuff that can overwhelm us. To think and feel like God has different rules is a form of pride. Feeling sorry for yourself and wanting attention is a form of idleness. You would never serve an idol, would you? I think feeling the way I was feeling was a type of idolatry. Anything against God is wrong. I looked back and see all the times in my life where I was blessed to get divine intervention. I told God, I felt like Mother Teresa did, having a different set of rules for me alone. I really have felt this way. I am sure if you have a disability or are a caregiver, you will get it. I knew this could not be true, so I saw what the Word had to say.

> Then Jesus said to the Jews who had believed in Him, "If you continue in My Word, you are truly My disciples and you will know the truth and the truth will make you free." (John 8:31–32)

> But He holds His priesthood permanently, because He continues forever. (Hebrews 7:24–25)

Consequently He is able, for all time, to save those who approach God through Him since He always lives to make intercession for them, even our disabilities.

Mercy triumphs judgment and love covers sin.

> For judgment will be without mercy to anyone who has shown no mercy; mercy triumphs over judgment. (James 2:13)

> Above all, maintain constant love for one another, for love covers a multitude of sins. Be hospitable to one another without complaining. Like good stewards of the manifold grace of God, serve one another with whatever gift each of you has received. (1 Peter 4:8–10)

I am asked all the time how I deal with it all. I tell them the truth which is, I live one day at a time and pray a lot. I live and an Isaiah-43 life. I pray all the time. "This the day the Lord has made; let us rejoice and be glad in it" (Psalms 118:24). If you do not know about Isaiah 43, you should read the whole chapter. Yes, the whole thing. It does not say "*if* the fires will burn you" or "*if* the water con-sumes you." It says when. Here is Isaiah 43.

> But now, this is what the Lord says—
> He who created you, Jacob,
> He who formed you, Israel:
> "Do not fear, for I have redeemed you;
> I have summoned you by name; you are mine.
> When you pass through the waters,
> I will be with you;
> and when you pass through the rivers,
> they will not sweep over you.
> When you walk through the fire,
> you will not be burned;
> the flames will not set you ablaze.
> For I am the Lord your God,
> the Holy One of Israel, your Savior;
> I give Egypt for your ransom,
> Cush and Seba in your stead.
> Since you are precious and honored in my sight,
> and because I love you,
> I will give people in exchange for you,
> nations in exchange for your life.
> Do not be afraid, for I am with you;
> I will bring your children from the east
> and gather you from the west.
> I will say to the north, 'Give them up!'
> and to the south, 'Do not hold them back.'
> Bring my sons from afar
> and my daughters from the ends of the earth—
> everyone who is called by my name,
> whom I created for my glory,
> whom I formed and made."
> Lead out those who have eyes but are blind,
> who have ears but are deaf.
> All the nations gather together

and the peoples assemble.
Which of their gods foretold this
and proclaimed to us the former things?
Let them bring in their witnesses to prove they were right,
so that others may hear and say, "It is true."
"You are my witnesses," declares the Lord,
"and my servant whom I have chosen,
so that you may know and believe me
and understand that I am He.
Before me no god was formed,
nor will there be one after me.
I, even I, am the Lord,
and apart from me there is no savior.
I have revealed and saved and proclaimed—
I, and not some foreign god among you.
"You are my witnesses," declares the Lord, "that I am God.
Yes, and from ancient days I am He.
No one can deliver out of my hand.
When I act, who can reverse it?"
God's mercy and Israel's unfaithfulness
This is what the Lord says—
Your Redeemer, the Holy One of Israel:
"For your sake I will send to Babylon
and bring down as fugitives all the Babylonians,
in the ships in which they took pride.
I am the Lord, your Holy One,
Israel's Creator, your King."
This is what the Lord says—
He who made a way through the sea,
a path through the mighty waters,
who drew out the chariots and horses,
the army and reinforcements together,
and they lay there, never to rise again,
extinguished, snuffed out like a wick:
"Forget the former things;
do not dwell on the past.

See, I am doing a new thing!
Now it springs up; do you not perceive it?
I am making a way in the wilderness
and streams in the wasteland.
The wild animals honor me,
the jackals and the owls,
because I provide water in the wilderness
and streams in the wasteland,
to give drink to my people, my chosen,
the people I formed for myself
that they may proclaim my praise.
Yet you have not called on me, Jacob,
you have not wearied yourselves for me, Israel.
You have not brought me sheep for burnt offerings,
nor honored me with your sacrifices.
I have not burdened you with grain offerings
nor wearied you with demands for incense.
You have not bought any fragrant calamus for me,
or lavished on me the fat of your sacrifices.
But you have burdened me with your sins
and wearied me with your offenses.
I, even I, am He who blots out
your transgressions, for my own sake,
and remembers your sins no more.
Review the past for me,
let us argue the matter together;
state the case for your innocence.
Your first father sinned;
those I sent to teach you rebelled against me.
So I disgraced the dignitaries of your temple;
I consigned Jacob to destruction
and Israel to scorn."

CHAPTER 7

I have begged God to not be disabled like Moses did for not being able to speak and someone who can handle it, someone else. Moses got his brother, Aaron, to speak. I got a disability. Great. Sometimes we do not get what we want and we are the one in our lives that can handle it. God must know what He is doing. Mystery. The reason why this happened to us, we might not know the reason. Doesn't that stink! He must know. That has been my experience. You must trust God. See we are ambassadors for God and must trust Him with a disability. We should be an example of all who we see, with and without a disability.

The hardest time of year for me is fall and all the holidays. I want to nest. I want to cook, clean, and decorate. I bet you do too if you are a woman with a disability. I did devotions earlier and would have rather been up earlier to do devotions and cook if I had no disability. I hate having a disability; I wish so bad to take care of my family and they have done it all, the cooking. You know how I started my day? Some devotions, catheter change, and diaper change. I swear, the hardest is being changed. I am still not used to it after years. I feel I will never get used to it! Did I say I hate having a disability? I tell Tim all the time, "This is not me, you know." I must sit back and ask for things I used to get myself. I want to be bossy but I cannot, in fear that I will push my family away. You can run your family away. I especially want to boss about the cooking, I guess that is the Sicilian in me! I do not usually fight with Tim. One day, he was making my pasta sauce and I thought he was taking too long. Well, I told him.

Listen, life never goes as planned. I can wish so hard life was different; it is not any different. I have had years of holidays and I still struggle. I try so hard to not think about holidays past when I had use of my body. I used to make my own ravioli. Thinking about the past holidays will not make it better. So I give the day to God and I will think of Him being next to me to get me through the day.

Remember to live one day at a time. Who knows what tomorrow will bring?

> You don't even know what tomorrow will bring. What is your life? For you are a mist that appears for a little while and then vanishes. Instead you ought to say, "If the Lord wishes, we will live and do this or that." (James 4:14–15)

> Therefore I tell you, do not worry about your life, what you will eat or drink, or about your body, what you will wear. Is not life more than food, and the body more than clothing? Look at the birds of the air; they neither sow not reap not gather in barns, and yet your heavenly Father feeds them. Are you not of more value than they? And can any of you by worrying add a single hour to your span of life? And why do you worry about clothing? Consider the lilies of the field, how they grow; they neither toil nor spin, yet I tell you even Solomon in all his glory was not clothed like one of these. But God so clothes the grass of the field, which is thrown into the oven, will he not much clothe you-you of little faith? Therefore, do not worry saying, "What will we eat?" Or "What will we drink?" or "What will we wear?" For it is the Gentiles who strive for all these things; and indeed, your heavenly Father knows what need all these things. But strive first for the kingdom of God and His righteousness, and all these things will be given to you a well. "So do not worry about tomorrow will bring worries of its own, Today's trouble is enough for today. (Matthew 6:25–34)

There is not one thing we can do to be get it. It is a free gift. "For the wages of sin is death, but the free gift of God is eternal life in Christ Jesus our Lord" (Romans 6:23). You can pray the rosary a million times or say the Our Father a million times and go to church a lot. You can even seek Him. Sometimes life is hard, we do not to think of that or talk about it. This is where bargaining can come in. You might say, "O God if I was healed, I would never complain again." Fill in the blanks for yourself. If you have a disability you have been here. If not, then good job.

One thing about the rosary I do not get, when you pray the Hail Marys and it says, "Blessed are you above all woman." She saw her Son mocked and crucified; as a mom, that must be hard. I think she is blessed *among* woman because she gets to be with Him forever in eternity and be the Mother of God. Now I can almost hear thoughts, *You pray the rosary?* I pray that Mary will pray for me like I have a friend pray for me. We ask for prayer in prayer chains and on Facebook. I pray to the Mother Mary because she can understand how hard it is being a mother and running a home. I think she gets it. It is hard with or without a disability, I see her as my advocate.

Just a note off the path. I bet she wonders why so many people put her in their gardens. Maybe to honor her. It is funny to me, at first, when I was learning how to do the rosary, I pictured Mary standing between me and God, like a protector saying, "Wait a second, she will die from all your holiness. She is unable to deal with it all, your power is so great, so just a minute." I think now, I know the rosary and picture her kneeling next to me and her arm is around me. We all forget God is still a King.

I love coffee but keep it out of church sanctuaries. God is the most important. Don't you think you should act and dress for a King. We do for weddings and reunions. It is not a concert or where I get fed. I give back to Him. It is the least we can do for Him. Some churches have the world behind them. How about a cross? A cross is not going to kill you! Churches are like a huge concert. I call them Fort God. I tell my girls we give up our comfort, and time for Him. It is just the least we do. Jesus is still personable and King at the same time.

I live now completely relying on the Lord. I experience some bad circumstance as you do too. According to the *Free Dictionary* online, *reliance* is defined as:

- The act of relying or the state of being reliant: *the economy's reliance on imported oil.*
- The faith, confidence, or trust felt by one who relies: *The general placed his reliance on the element of surprise.*
- See Synonyms at *trust*. *Archaic* One relied on; a mainstay.

Stability as defined as:

- The state or quality of being stable, especially. Resistance to change, deterioration, or displacement. Constancy of character or purpose; steadfastness.
- Reliability; dependability. The ability of an object, such as a ship or aircraft, to maintain equilibrium or resume its original, upright position after displacement, as by the sea or strong winds.
- *Roman Catholic Church* A vow committing a Benedictine monk to one monastery for life.

Talk about trusting God. I had been recovering from an infection, and Tim quit his job and he had to look for a home for us to work at a church and homeless mission in Michigan. We packed blind, not having a place to live. Were we freaking out? Yes, big-time. With me being in a wheelchair, we had to find a wheelchair-accessible. We ended up finding a new apartment that was wheelchair-accessible. I even was able to keep our dog and the landlord does not allow pets. You never know what God has planned. We packed our house blind. We packed our house not having a job for Tim and a place to live. So many people have been praying for us to find a home. Did I complain? Why yes! I was so uncomfortable.

Trust in the Lord with all your heart,
and do not rely on your own insight.

In all your ways acknowledge Him,
and He will make straight your paths.
Do not be wise in your own eyes;
fear the Lord, and turn away from evil.
It will be a healing for your flesh
and a refreshment for your body. (Proverbs 3:5–8)

I have no healing or refreshment. I still have disabilities. I do not rely on my own understanding. Come on, I cannot be the only one to feel this way. I survive to have God in my life, and I feel better if He knows what is going on with me. He knows before I say a word.

There is a prayer of St. Chrysostom. It goes as followed:

> Almighty God, who hast given us grace at this time with one accord to make our common supplication unto thee; and hast promised through thy well-beloved Son that when two or three are gathered together in his Name thou wilt be in the midst of them: Fulfill now, O Lord, the desires and petitions of thy servants as may be best for us; granting us in this world knowledge of thy truth, and in the world to come life everlasting.

I like the part it says, "Fulfill now, O Lord, the desires and petitions of thy servants as best for us." As best for us. He sees all our life; He knows better than we do what is best for us. If we were healed right this second, it might not be in our best interest. You might say, how can disability be okay with God? I am not saying that, okay? Simmer down now. With a disability, I have to rely that God knows what He is doing. I have no idea what I am doing, thank goodness He does.

I remember one time when my friend and I rang bells for the Salvation Army in Tampa, Florida, and got paid to do it. It was nice to be so close to the ocean. My friend and I went to Disney, and a group of Swedish guys were taking my picture and I caught them and asked why. They said their country does not many brunettes. They took selfies with me and they thought I was pretty and gave me a Mickey balloon. I was flattered.

In college, some of us would ring bells for the Salvation Army. It was fun, and some of us got to ring in St. Petersburg, Florida. It was so cool because we would go to the beach at the times we were not working. My friend and I buried a guy in sand, and then we put shells to make it look like he had breasts. The funniest was when I threw Cheetos on him (not on his face or eyes), all the seagulls came to eat them but he was not able to move. We laughed because he screamed like a girl.

We saw where the money in those little red buckets go at the Salvation Army—food packages for needy families. I saw this and will always donate to them. I was trying to catch a plane form Tampa to Detroit. This was before 9/11 and the checks were not very strict like they are nowadays. We were running late for the plane and a terminal shuttle bus left. I thought it was a good idea to run to the plane. So we were left running, with my luggage in tow, to the plane. I remember running and going through a door marked "No Entry." I did not hear the alarm, all I thought of was getting to the plane; you would get arrested these days. I made the plane! I was embarrassed and thought I would never see them again.

I rang bells in Pontiac, Michigan, and it was so cold, and my friend and I kept on getting the stomach flu more than once. We had a team meeting and the leader told all of us to use different bathrooms from the boys. We were told the boys had the bathroom down the stairs and the girls had the same-floor bathrooms. He told us there were no exceptions, they said they were strict about this. I saw my friend go into our bathroom, and I was going to have some fun with her. I followed her into the bathroom and flicked the light on and off as I sang "Disco Duck." I then threw water over every stall, and I kicked in the stall, saying, "Hiya." And she was laughing. Then I saw him as I yelled, "Hiya!

I saw a guy who was all red and wet with his feet up. He knew he was not to be in there. He had gotten the stomach flu too. This poor guy! I did all this to him too. I am sure he never forgot this. He did not have eye contact with me after that. I do not blame him.

It was funny to my friend and me and embarrassing to him. I was embarrassed for doing all that to him. I was not going to tell on him. I can see it play in my head now, and it is still funny to me.

I picture God working with me like me cliff diving. I used to cliff dive at Lake Harrington in my summers during college. The cliffs were not high, and I was still chicken. I wonder what I was thinking. In college, you think you are invincible—you are not. I picture going to a cliff and God catching me. Now it not easy to get to a cliff God has. I picture myself having to be dragged to the edge. I would fight with God and would not want to go. A big decision had to be made: Was I going to allow God work or not? Was I going to obey or not? I would get to an edge God has for me and look down at an endless cliff, scary at the bottom and would not want to jump and trust God to catch me at the end. When I got to the edge, had to jump for God to work with me. There was no turning back. It is kind of like being in a roller-coaster line and no turning back.

A funny and true story, my cousin and I went on a fair ride called The Zipper. Someone got sick and I said, in a funny way, to watch out for the pink vomit. It turned out it was my cousin who got sick riding next to me.

Back to cliff diving. You get to an edge and make a choice to jump, trusting God to catch you when you do not know what is at the bottom. Jumping, I imagine a crisis of some sort. What do you do? Imagine. I am sure God has worked with you. When you fall, you flail your arms and scream; it does not feel good at all. You can even hit the sharp sides. You wonder if it (crisis) will even end. This is the part where I feel like I rely totally on God. This the part where I really pray. When you go through bad times, at the very least, you have God to go though it with you. You get your nerves to walk this life on earth with God.

God understands your flailing, screaming, and fear, hitting sides. I think He just knows how you feel. You get to the bottom and God catches you, just in time; you think you will never be caught. You made it through a hard and bad time and learned some things about yourself and God. It is at this point you are stronger than you think and there is a purpose.

I felt my disability was like this. To me, everything gets worse like sharp edges from the cliff. I was still disabled and did not like it. I am a more mature Christian for it. If there was no disability, I would have not learned many things.

> I fed you with milk, and not solid food. For you were not ready for solid food, even now you are not ready. (1 Corinthians 3:2)

> About this we have much to say that is hard to explain, since you became dull in understanding. For through this time you should be teachers, you need someone to teach again the basic elements of the oracles of God. You need milk not solid food; for everyone who lives on milk, for everyone who lives on milk, being still an infant, is unskilled in the word of righteousness. But solid food is for the mature, for those who faculties have been trained by practice to distinguish good from evil. (Hebrews 5:11–14)

Do not feel bad, I like the milk. We all learn from making mistakes and still have the consequences. Don't you hate that! We do not want the consequences. They are not fun to have. This is how we learn. Each day, I think to myself, *This could be the day I am healed.* But I am not. It is hard to follow God when you have a permanent disability or a caregiver can feel the same because their life is affected too. There were two songs that I can think of God telling me stuff. In 1992, a song by the Disney movie *Aladdin* came out, and I graduated from college in 1993 and just knew my future was going to be amazing. I made it through college. I believe the lyrics were God's message to me. College and social work allowed me to do that. Even now, with being disabled, I still feel it as my calling. Here are the lyrics to "A Whole New World." The second song was by Alicia Keys. "Only You" makes me think of God. I imagined my song from God to me.

I think God knows who will follow His ways and live by His statures like the narrow path. God knows who will choose the narrow path and who will not. I like the following scriptures:

> Do not let loyalty and faithfulness forsake you; bind them around your neck, write them on the tablet of your heart. So you will find favor and good repute in the sight of God and of people. Trust in the Lord with all your heart, and do not rely on your own insight. In all your ways acknowledge him and he will make straight your paths. (Proverbs 3:3–6)

> Enter through the narrow gate; for the gate is wide and the road is easy that leads to destruction, and there are many who take it. For the gate is narrow and the road is hard that leads to life, and there are few who find it. (Mathew 7:13–14)

See? It is much easier to walk this life on earth entering through the wide gate. If we, as disabled, walk the narrow gate, God must think we can handle it. Being disabled is a hard life to live, everything we do has to be adjusted and there are some things we just cannot do. I think of the narrow gate and the wide gate are a way we can live. The narrow gate to me is always to live without sin. We try to please God and keep all His commandments. The ways of the world are the wide gate to me. It is like the world we live in ways, has sin. The world's ways seem distorted. Much harder. We must endure and persevere. We must not get tired from doing good. In this world is much good, we are different. The Bible says we live our daily life different from the world. Walking through the narrow gate and path is not doing what you feel with disability. Look at the Nicene Creed, here it is:

> We believe in one God,
> The Father, the Almighty,
> Maker of heaven and earth,

Of all that is, seen and unseen.
We believe in one Lord, Jesus Christ,
The only Son of God,
Eternally begotten of the Father,
God from God, Light from Light,
True God from true God,
Begotten, not made,
Of one Being with the Father.
Through Him all things were made.
For us and for our salvation
He came down from heaven:
By the power of the Holy Spirit
He became incarnate from the Virgin Mary,
And was made man.
For our sake He was crucified under Pontius Pilate;
He suffered death and was buried.
On the third day He rose again
In accordance with the Scriptures;
He ascended into heaven
And is seated at the right hand of the Father.
He will come again in glory to judge the living and the dead,
And His kingdom will have no end.
We believe in the Holy Spirit, the Lord, the giver of life,
Who proceeds from the Father and the Son.
With the Father and the Son He is worshiped and glorified.
He has spoken through the Prophets.
We believe in one holy catholic and apostolic Church.
We acknowledge one baptism for the forgiveness of sins.
We look for the resurrection of the dead
And the life of the world to come. Amen.

I like this creed and use the handout to read it because it says the Apostles Creed every day and I get them confused with each other. Disability, we must accept being uncomfortable.

God understands emotions. God has feelings, He understands emotions like jealousy, compassion, and here, anger. I am too chicken to even ask why. Read the last chapter of Job and you will be humbled, so things are just a mystery. We will not always have the answers.

> The Passover of the Jews was near, and Jesus went up to Jerusalem. In the temple he found people selling cattle, sheep, and doves, and the money changers seated at their tables. Making a whip of cords, he drove all of them out of the temple, both the sheep and the cattle. He also poured out the coins of the money changers and overturned their tables. He told those who were selling the doves, "Take these things out of here! Stop making my Father's house a marketplace!" His disciples remembered that it was written, "Zeal for your house will consume me." The Jews then said to him, "What sign can you show us for doing this?" Jesus answered them, "Destroy this temple, and in three days I will raise it up." The Jews then said, "This temple has been under construction for forty-six years, and will you raise it up in three days?" But he was speaking of the temple of his body. After he was raised from the dead, his disciples remembered that he had said this; and they believed the scripture and the word that Jesus had spoken. (John 6:13–22)

Can you accept mysteries? It is a large part of Christianity.

> He has made known to us the mystery of His will, according to His good pleasure that He set forth in Christ. (Ephesians 1:9)

> And how the mystery was made known to me by revelation, as I wrote above in a few words, a reading of which will enable you to perceive my understanding of the mystery of Christ. In

former generations, this mystery was not made
known to humankind, as it has not been revealed
to His holy apostles and prophets by the Spirit.
(Ephesians 3:3–5)

When you feel nothing is ever going to change, is the place I
find, where you are used the most by God. I think further and deeper
than hopelessness. You have not a thing go the way you want it to go,
feels bad. Hopelessness is bad, I was taught in clinical social work;
but it really does happen, and it appears others are afraid to mention
or talk about it. It is a real feeling. I think Jesus on the cross felt forsaken and hopelessness too.

I do not agree that hopelessness means suicide. I think it is a red
flag to us that there is something wrong going on. It must happen to
some of us. Right? *Despair* is a good word at this point because it is
worse than hopelessness. I love the next scripture because we do not
have be in despair.

But we have this treasure in clay jars, so that it
may be made clear that this extraordinary power
belongs to God and does not come from us. We
are afflicted in every way, but not crushed; per-
plexed, but not driven to Despair; persecuted,
but not forsaken; struck down, but not destroyed;
always carrying in the body the death of Jesus, so
that the life of Jesus may also be made visible in
our bodies. For while we live, we are always being
given up to death for Jesus' sake, so that the life
of Jesus may be made visible in our mortal flesh.
So death is at work in us, but life in you, I sure
felt hopeless and despair when I got disabled. (2
Corinthians 4:7–12)

Our God is our God today, right now. God delights in us, look
at the following scripture, "His delight is not in the strength of the
horse, nor his pleasure in the speed of a runner; but the Lord takes

pleasure in those who fear him, in those who hope in his steadfast love" (Psalms 147:10–11). We are His possession. I guess you are thinking, *I am no one's possession.* I take comfort He is on my side and I am a possession of His. We take care of our possessions and treasure them, right? He has clemency for us. I had to look up *clemency*, I had never heard it before. The *Webster's* dictionary online says what it means: "disposition to be merciful and especially to moderate the severity of punishment due, "The judge ignored the prisoner's pleas for *clemency*." An act or instance of leniency.

There are times we must pause and take a break. I think he knows us better than we do. Selah is important, it is just a part of a name in my book. In the Word, Selah is in the online Wikipedia:

> Selah (/ˈsiːlə/ or /ˈsiːləh/ with pronounced audible H; Hebrew: סֶלָה, also transliterated as *selāh*) is a word used seventy-four times in the Hebrew Bible—seventy-one times in the Psalms and three times in Habakkuk. The meaning of the word is not known, though various interpretations are given below. (It should not be confused with the Hebrew word *sela'* (Hebrew: סֶלַע) which means "rock", or in an adjectival form, "like a rock", i.e.: firm, hard, heavy, as in Sela Public Charter School) It is probably either a liturgical-musical mark or an instruction on the reading of the text, something like "stop and listen." *Selah* can also be used to indicate that there is to be a musical interlude at that point in the Psalm. The Amplified Bible translates *selah* as "pause, and think of that." It can also be interpreted as a form of underlining in preparation for the next paragraph.
>
> At least some of the Psalms were sung accompanied by musical instruments and there are references to this in many chapters. Thirty-one of the thirty-nine psalms with the caption

"To the choir-master" include the word *selah*.
Selah may indicate a break in the song whose purpose is similar to that of Amen (Hebrew: "so be it") in that it stresses the truth and importance of the preceding passage; this interpretation is consistent with the meaning of the Semitic root *ṣ-l-ḥ* also reflected in Arabic cognate *salih* (variously "valid" [in the logical sense of "truth-preserving"], "honest," and "righteous"). Altermely, *selah* may mean "forever," as it does in some places in the liturgy (notably the second to last blessing of the Amidah). Another interpretation claims that *selah* comes from the primary Hebrew root word *salah* (סָלָה) which means "to hang," and by implication to measure (weigh).

The Lord was with Joseph and showed him steadfast love; he showed him favor in the sight of the chief jailer. The chief jailer committed to Joseph's care all the prisoners who were in the prison, and whatever done there, here (Joseph) was the one to do it. The chief jailer paid no heed to anything in Joseph's care, because the Lord was with him; and whatever he did, the Lord made it prosper. (Genesis 39:21–23)

I believe God could take something bad in our lives and make it good eventually. God could even make us prosper with a disability. When others talk about prosper, it is about money. There are other things that can be prosperous. Make a time line of your life and where God has worked, you will notice God hears your prayers and He has been working hard on your life. Hard to think of when you live with a permanent disability. God sees all our suffering; God is watching over us.

Let me ask you something, if you know you are going through a hard time, would you not want to go through it with God and not alone?

> The Lord was with Joseph and showed him stead-
> fast love; he showed him favor in the sight of the
> chief jailer. The chief jailer committed to Joseph's
> care all the prisoners who were in the prison, and
> whatever done there, here (Joseph) was the one
> to do it. The chief jailer paid no heed to anything
> in Joseph's care, because the Lord was with him;
> and whatever he did, the Lord made it prosper.
> (Genesis 39:21–23)

I believe God could take something bad in our lives and make it good eventually. God could even make us prosper with a disability. When others talk about prosper, it is about money. There are other things that can be prosperous.

Things can change in a second; a disability will do that like we cannot control stuff. I will give a great some example. In 2012, we had tornado that wiped the town we lived in Kentucky totally out. I have never seen so much damage. Tim was singing to the girls and dog, all in the hall bathroom. He was trying to keep all calm. My chair would not fit in the bathroom, and till this day, I do not know what the hall bathroom looks like. The girls will take pictures for me of things I don't get to see. I was amazed at the tornado. We cracked our windows and I heard the blinds being sucked out and in. Here Tim was trying to keep all calm, and I kept saying, "Do you hear that?" It was two tornados that turned into one. People lost their lives. Sad. You can google it online to see the tornado if you want to. We had one earlier in the week on a Wednesday (what are the chances of a tornado in Appalachia, two times). I was on the phone with my sister Amy and she heard it and asked what all the noise was I said wind and trees. The girls were at school late due to the bad weather, and I was talking to my sister and the power went out and I had nothing to do so I dusted. This was before the stroke and

I figured if the house blew away, it would be dusted. I just had a bad feeling that day in March when the tornados hit.

I got ready. I canceled my hair appointment, got the girls from school early, and even gassed up and oil changed the car. I had a pick line of antibiotic and got all my medicines and got a cooler ready. The best thing I did was have everyone pack for three days. We had no power for five days and found a place to stay that would take our dog with us. We live in a soup bowl, hard to get a cell connection here. Like we can have some sort of control. If the weather got bad, I would watch the news. I worried trees would fall on the house. A tree fell once, and Grace took some pictures. Like I could control the weather or the trees. I felt I had some control if I had knowledge.

I had a lady bathe me twice a week and had a stranger come and bathe me this week. Listen, I did not care because I was so thankful to be bathed other than my husband. There I was, in a T-shirt and someone new. She said it was getting hot and fell and had a seizure. I yelled for the girls to come and help. Grace caught her and laid her on her left side, and I had Hope lock Lilly in the room and to look in her purse for a cell phone so we could call 9-1-1, and then her husband. I told the girls, "We can panic later, right now, this lady needs us."

Hope flagged down the first responders and we found her cell and called 9-1-1. I was not able to do a thing but boss them around. It is embarrassing when you know the first responders! "Hi, it is me again, but I am not septic." I went to see her at the hospital with the family but she had already gone home. She no longer worked for home health anymore. I know that means life-interrupted crisis will come. It came to her and those that loved her.

There is a song by Chris Tomlin called "Jesus." Here are the words:

> There is a truth older than the ages
> There is a promise of things yet to come
> There is one, born for our salvation
> Jesus
> There is a light that overwhelms the darkness
> There is a kingdom that forever reigns

There is freedom from the chains that bind us
Jesus, Jesus
Who walks on the waters
Who speaks to the sea
Who stands in the fire beside me
He roars like a lion
He bled as the lamb
He carries my healing in his hands
Jesus
There is a name I call in times of trouble
There is a song that comforts in the night
There is a voice that calms the storm that rages
He is Jesus, Jesus
Who walks on the waters
Who speaks to the sea
Who stands in the fire beside me
He roars like a lion
He bled as the lamb
He carries my healing in his hands
Jesus
Messiah, my Savior
There is power in Your name
You're my rock and, my redeemer
There is power in Your name
In Your name
You walk on the waters
You speak to the sea
You stand in the fire beside me
You roar like a lion
You bled as the lamb
You carry my healing in Your hands
God, you walk on the waters
You speak to the sea
You stand in the fire beside me
You roar like a lion
You bled as the lamb

You carry my healing in Your hands
Jesus
There is no one like you
Jesus
There is no one like you

I like it so much, for all He has done for me. I get choked up
when I look back on life and where I see where God has been working. I am an optimist and think God made me resilient. The following story is all over the Internet:

> A family had twin boys whose only resemblance
> to each other was their looks. If one felt it was
> too hot, the other thought it was too cold. If one
> said the TV was too loud, the other claimed the
> volume needed to be turned up. Opposite in
> every way, one was an eternal optimist, the other
> a doom & gloom pessimist.
>
> Just to see what would happen, on the
> twins' birthday their father loaded the pessimist's
> room with every imaginable toy and game. The
> optimist's room he loaded with horse manure.
>
> That night the father passed by the pessi-
> mist's room and found him sitting amid his new
> gifts crying bitterly.
>
> "Why are you crying?" the father asked.
>
> "Because my friends will be jealous, I'll
> have to read all these instructions before I can do
> anything with this stuff, I'll constantly need bat-
> teries, and my toys will eventually get broken,"
> answered the pessimist twin.
>
> Passing the optimist twin's room, the father
> found him dancing for joy in the pile of manure.
> "What are you so happy about?" he asked.
>
> To which his optimist twin replied, "There's
> got to be a pony in here somewhere!"

Tim and I took vows before God and meant it. "Sickness and in health," we had to walk. Boy, did we ever had to walk that. We balance each other out. If I had to be with someone just like I am, I would most likely want to hurt them. I met Tim in August 1994, and by October 1994, we were engaged and a ring on my finger. We were married in May 1994; now that was fast. I would freak out if I knew someone getting married so fast.

I was at a wedding once, and my dad was so happy and proud of Tim, he made him get in all the pictures and told everyone we were getting married! I did not have a ring on yet! It was the bride's day. I joked with Tim and told him he was stuck with me now! We have been married years, and he says no matter how hard it gets he will always love me. Disability has been so hard on him.

I met him at a church I was visiting, and our cars were the same color and parked next to each other. It is important to know the night before, I prayed to God; I was done looking for a spouse and would be happy alone, and that same night, the lady I babysat for prayed for me to find a spouse. I felt led and my friend felt strongly we should go to visit a church we have never been to. I got in and saw a guy wearing a white shirt praying hard. I told my friend to look and said to I wanted a guy like that. It was Tim. He looks so good in the color white.

Church was done and we went to our cars, and he turned his car around to talk to us. I thought he was there for my pretty friend. They always wanted to meet my pretty friends. I got used to it. But he turned his car around to talk to me. The guy in the white shirt, praying to God, came to talk to me. He followed us home to Wilmore, Kentucky. Our town was so small, and at this time, we only had one light. I told my friend if the light turns red, she can jump out and ask him over to my apartment for lunch. I could not believe he was interested in me.

I had always learned a way to a man's heart is through his stomach! Maybe the Sicilian in me. We had lunch, and he asked me out. The morning of our first date, I almost canceled, and a strong thought said for me to, *Let him love you! Don't you dare cancel!* We fell in love fast, and I knew from the first date, I would marry this man. There were other girls that liked him and said they were just "friends." I was not going to fight and told him I was the only girl he would like, and if he had these other girls like him, I was outta here. It is just like Tim to have no idea when girls are after him.

I thought he was one created for me and I for him. By the way, I got great in-laws. I was so independent; I had my own job, car, and home. I told poor Tim, I told him I was not going to change and he could not take away all the things I worked hard for. It came out of nowhere for Tim. When it was time to get married, my grandma put pennies in my shoes and said a Sicilian blessing, and my dad said he was not giving me up. My dad said he could not give up his daughter and was going to entrust me to Tim. I think he knew we were created for each other. We have been married for many years. I cannot remember any time when we ever called each other names or swore at each other. I know he is smart, but I admired his nice side and his ability to be kind to everyone at any time. He does not see it, but I do. He is genuinely empathetic. If he has a problem with another, I think to myself, *They must have a problem because Tim is a peacemaker.*"

I tell him all the time, he does more than most guys would do. He does what does not feel like doing. He does well at taking care of me. He must do everything for me. I was high-maintenance, even more now. I wanted to look my best, no matter what has happened. I was determined to be the best I could be in a chair and with a speech problem. Since I got a disability, I carried weight in my stomach; with a disability, your body changes too.

CHAPTER 8

I get treated so different than before. People will ignore me or give me too much attention. Nobody knows what to do with me. I can understand this. I love it when others treat me like they did before. I had bad things happen to me. I had a lady try to be nice and said to me, in a baby-talk voice, "Good job on your makeup." I was nice because, in her way, she was trying to be nice. I even have to bribe kids to not be afraid of me. With a disability, it can scare kids because they do not see it often. Before my stroke, I would give kids a ride or push the buttons on my wheelchair. With the stroke, my arms are weaker, I just cannot do it. So I resort to bribing, and so far, it works.

You know what I don't like? I don't like it when people park in the handicapped parking when they don't need it. Others who have big trucks or others with kids and have no visible handicap. I have a place in the front of my car where my chair fits, and I get mean looks from others. When I get out and stared at by the people in handicapped parking, they tend to look like they feel guilty. Not my intention at all. I want them to think about parking there if not needed. It is none of my business. I say hi to them and I get ignored. I know they see me. How can they not? I am the one whose chair makes noise, and I am in a wheelchair. I am kind of hard to miss. Tim, my husband, sees this all the time, and it is hard on him to see.

I do not like to ask for help and struggle to ask; I need a lot of help. Follow God no matter how bad our circumstances get. I just cannot throw my whole experiences away. God has been faithful in the past. "But those who have doubts are condemned if they if they eat, because they do not act from faith; for whatever dose not proceed from faith is sin, this is no different" (Romans 14:23). It has taken longer for God to act—years. I feel like crawling in a hole.

My wheelchair van broke down. This is huge for me, do not get to go to Mass, the girls' events, or doctor appointments. I am homebound. I do not get a choice; I need that van. I do not get to get out to even shop. I had to ask for help to get a new wheelchair van. I do not like to ask for help often, and here I am, asking for help to get one. I want to fade into the background. I want no attention, but here I am, for all to see. There is a GoFundMe for a new van for me. People are so generous, and I have a down payment for one.

I used to be able to take care of my family. Now they must help; sometimes the children must drain out my catheter. I would not normally have them do this. If it does not get drained, it could back up and cause me another stroke. There have been many times I had to go through a drive-through and order a drink and dump it out to drain my catheter. What others take for granted, you and your caregivers think about. And you look at the ramps wherever you go. Even a simple door can be a challenge. Now I needed help.

I used to teach Sunday school and hold the calash full of wine to offer. I was afraid at first because I was thinking, *I saw the ending of* Indiana Jones *where all the Nazi faces melted off.* I can barely hold a cup now! I love to attend Mass and I sit in the front row. If you have a disability or a caregiver, you have to sit in front rows of places like movies and church.

My body will sometimes shut down on me with no warning. I fell asleep in Mass and woke up to my daughter Hope waking me up and me snoring. Embarrassing, right? I was determined to never let my body shut down. It is like having your first child. You must make sure you have everything. I would have to make sure to have my catheter drainer and make sure I am dressed right because I struggle with temperatures. I must be sure I can fit into places, even places that have a ramp. I must make sure the door does not have a lip.

Tim and I went up to Oscoda, Michigan, to have Tim preach and for us to go to an open house in a wheelchair-accessible home. I liked my chair can go on the boardwalk on the beach. Another tip to Oscoda, Michigan, our air conditioner in our car broke and it was sunny and 97 degrees out. I do not sweat from being paralyzed but I get hot and really quiet. Tim said I looked flushed and not so good.

I told him I was hot, he got me to cool air and some to drink. I did not want to pass out in front of others. Tim got me drinks, a new T-shirt, and ice packs to put under my armpits. When we got home, I was still warm. Tim took a body temperature and I was up to 101.6 and that is even when I was in air conditioning. It goes with being paralyzed; now I know I can overheat.

My chair does not work in sand. Instead of getting upset I could not lay on the beach and soak up the sun, I choose to focus on what I can do. It is important, with a disability, to focus on what you can do more than what you cannot do. If you do not, then you can get angry and depressed.

I know how hard it is to have a disability. I was in my bedroom and broke my TV and the big mirror on my dresser fell but did not break. I saw it happening in slow motion and tried to prevent them from falling. I tried to catch them with my arms and hands. My hands and arms are weak from the stroke and I drop things often. I am used to it. It made a loud noise, and Tim came running. I was more upset my TV broke because I like TV. Things are going to happen and not in your power to control it with disability.

The hardest is when you want no attention and fade in the background and you can't. You going anywhere is a production. It just is because others want to make you as comfortable possible. I like the show *Speechless*; it comes on at 8:30 p.m. on Wednesday night. They have a son who is disabled and is always late. If you have a disability, you know it can be hard to be at places on time. I cannot get up and go; I have my blood lowered if I try. Tim and I figured out how to get to places on time by trial and error. On this show, the disabled boy and his caregiver learned that they were "inspirational" everywhere they go. They did not have to wait in line, all acted nice to them, and they got free stuff. The boy with the disability got sick of it and told the caregiver to stop. The caregiver thought it was great before he was told not to do that/it. I get that stuff now, and it bothers me because I want fade in the background.

One time, Tim and I surprised the girls and went to see *Harry Potter Deathly Hollows, Part 1*. My nephew, TJ, was there in a long line. My family and I were brought in and seated first because of my disability. I even got a box to put earrings in for a Christmas and asked, in my new voice, if they had a box. The lady behind the counter said she did not. I was happy to be treated normal. The other lady behind the counter looked at her and gave a look that said, "Really, give her one." I then mistakenly drove my chair into the watch counter. It has been eight years and I still bang into things. It made a loud noise, and I was embarrassed. I told Tim we only got a box because I was in a chair. I pay attention to something else and run into things too much.

Do you ever think God has already dealt with you and your problems before? I feel like nothing is a surprise for Him. The illnesses and problems are not a shock to Him. He must know how disability turns our lives upside down and we must find a new normal. "For we are what he has made us, created in Christ Jesus for good works, which God prepared beforehand to be our way of life" (Ephesians 2:10). See it is even in the Bible.

I was paralyzed and was on so many medicine, I was embarrassed. My medicine list was two pages. When I was first paralyzed, I tried to do everything you can imagine to not face all I went through. In 2014, I was prepared to face it all. Denial, remember. I noticed when the medications wore off, I would have withdrawal symptoms. I had to get off those. Those were not good. When you get paralyzed and feel pain, you have many medications prescribed. I would wake up at night and cry. Tim would see me and then took Ambien to sleep. It works for some people, just not me. My family and I would call me, when I had it. Ambien Anna. I would take it and be unreliable and out of my mind. I was reading the book *The Hunger Games* when I was on it. The book kept on falling on my face and I told Tim the book was broken—I was falling asleep!

I gave my daughter Hope twenty dollars for lunch. I was convinced I could walk, and Tim saw me try to get out of bed on several different occasions to try and walk. Poor Tim, I told Tim I hated the hospital bed and we did not snuggle as much since I was injured. He got smashed into my small hospital bed and snuggled me and I asked him how long he was planning to stay. I must have been more comfortable being alone.

God knows what is best. He knows the desires of our hearts. I have an in dwelling catheter. What a mess. I tried to straight cath. My arms would not let me, and I made a huge mess. It causes trouble that comes in the form of infection, sepsis, and E. coli, C-Diff. Of course, I would not want this. I do not blame Jesus for praying this in the garden of Gethsemane. I would die if I was being crucified (literally). I do not know how He did it; I could never. You know, at any time, He could show His power but did not. Why when chief priests and the Pharisees fell when Jesus was arrested, all fell? It is never talked about. It is not in any movies. Look it up.

> Then Jesus, knowing all that was to happen to him, came forward and asked them, "Whom are you looking for?" They answered, "Jesus of Nazareth. Jesus replied, "I am he." Judas, who betrayed him, was standing with them. When Jesus said to them, "I am he," they stepped back and fell to the ground. Again he asked them, "Whom are you looking for?" And they said, "Jesus of Nazareth." Jesus answered, "I told you that I am he. So, if you are looking for me, let these men go." (John 18:4–8)

My body was addicted to prescribed pain medicine; at the same time, I was even teaching a Bible study on strongholds! So I hungered down in my room and pridefully thought I could handle going cold turkey. Boy, did I learn the hard way though. I really thought I could handle it with no help. I got wine, chocolate, sleeping pills, and funny shows on television. I hid from all and tried to hide it from my kids. It was the worst pain I ever felt; the air hurt! Air! I suffered greatly and wanted God to take it away. I was feeling hopeless, and I thought I would never get off OxyContin and the fentanyl patch.

I tried to cut down the medicine on my own. I failed over and over. I thought going cold turkey, I was doing something right, and if I needed God, I really needed Him. I was suffering. Suffering bad and wanted God to take it away. I did a repeated motion with my arms. It was not God's fault. I was the one who had taken the medicine.

I remembered Tim calling the first responders and must have passed out because I never heard the sirens and did not feel a thing. I later woke up at the hospital. They said I had seizures and my heart stopped. I had no idea. I saw my lip was cut and saw double. Tim said when my heart stopped, he said the doctor jumped on top of me and did CPR. How dramatic. It was like something on television, I went through a bad withdrawal that caused auto dysreflexia and had a stroke.

If you are septic, most will never survive. I was blessed to be alive. The woman next to me had the television and wanted to have it on all the time, country gospel. I wanted to watch the *Big Bang Theory*, I even dreamt a nurse came in and told the lady next to me it was a funny show. If you are Septic, you are out of your mind. Completely out of your mind. I thought Jennifer Lopez was my best friend, Doctor Oz was treating me, and I was at a different hospital. Oh, I even thought the second floor of the hospital had lots of therapy dogs being feed Whoppers from Burger King. I was so worried about them and told Tim all about this.

Another thing it thought, I thought I met President Obama. He was at the University of Kentucky and was on the news during this time. I told Tim all about it. I thought I really met him. I made up this guy named Paul P. I thought he was in the hospital to hurt me and rape me. I thought he was shot by his wife who knew of his plans. I thought I heard him breathing and made all who entered my room to check under my bed. Okay, I watch too much of *Days of Our Lives*. I must have been persuasive because anyone who entered my room would check and found nothing, trying to convince me. It was my neighbor in the bed next to me, breathing and snoring. Remember I was septic. I yelled quotes form the movie *Braveheart*. "You can't take my freedom!" I must have yelled "Freedom!" too much, they marked on my wall under a paper.

I was afraid of men. I heard them present my case to other professionals, saying I was afraid of men. I even thought I had to go to jail and to prison for a week. I thought I was and told Tim I had to go to jail and then to prison for a week. I was so sorry; in my head, I knew it would be hard on those who loved me. I thought Paul was going to the same prison. I got ready in my mind to fight him or harm him. In my head, I went to prison for a week. I was so sick.

I have a theory about addiction. All those who were addicted physically and mentally hate to go through withdrawal. Withdrawal hurts very bad, and it is the worst pain ever. I heard the phrase, "Kick the bucket" because you look like you are kicking a bucket repeatedly. Those who have an addiction want to stop but are not able to.

Okay, back to my theory. Those who are mentally addicted will lie, cheat, and steal to not go through withdrawal. I think they will do anything to those they love because they think their loved ones will hate to see them in withdrawal. Withdrawal is so bad. You cannot tell others accurately how bad it is unless you have had it yourself. Those with addiction need love, mercy, and compassion. Mercy triumphs judgement, only the drug or withdrawal will help. Do not be prideful like me and try to handle it yourself. You just cannot.

I got moved to a different floor of the hospital and was told by my doctor I had a stroke. I did not believe my doctor. I told him I was too young and told him he was lying. He had to show me on the MRI film where I had a stroke. He said I used to have a ventilator to help me breath and was tied down. I was going to leave at this time and tried to pull the tubes out. I do not remember being tied down. Thank God! I thought maybe I could get some rest. I was moved and felt like I had no rest.

I had OT, PT, and SP. I had respiratory therapists, medicine, nurses, doctors, caregivers and visitors. I just wanted to be left alone to sleep—I needed and wanted sleep. I did all they told me to do so they would leave me alone. I thought I was going to die and no one would tell me. So I told this to a nurse all what I thought I knew and I watched the movie *Nemo*. My nurse did her charting on the computer, next to my bed, standing up. I wanted to go home. I was moved to another floor. The lady in the room next to me died and her son and husband were angry and gave the poor nurses an earful. I did not know what to do for everyone who was sad.

When you do not know what to do, do what you know to do—pray—and do it again, talk to God. I had no control, and I was not strong. Control, like there is such a thing. If you have a disability, there is no control. When you have a code called, everyone comes to your room. I told them I did not know any of them and asked why they were there. I did not remember the codes at all. I told them I was not going home, was I? Oh, I wanted to go home so bad so I could sleep. I was stuck there for a month. I was moved every two hours and had no real sleep. I had a fan and slept sitting up to breathe and did everything they would say so they would leave me alone. I was not going to die and could go home. *Finally*, I thought. *My own bed, TV, and Tim and the girls.*

My poor family. This I could not hide. I had lots of home care. My arms were so weak and I could not do much. I used to be able to roll side to side in my bed. I sleep so still on my back, I could not read or write anymore. The letters to anything I read looked smashed. One thing I like to do is watch TV. I get tired so easily. I see double when I get tired. After the stroke, everything changed so much. I had to learn simple stuff again like breathe. If you listen to me closely, you will hear and see me run out of air and breathe in again. I had to learn how to swallow so I did not choke, and my voice was different and I would get confused often.

CHAPTER 9

Easter is my favorite holiday. I spent Easter weekend in Jupiter, Florida, at my friend's house. Her dad worked for NASA, and they had a lemon and grapefruit tree in their yard. I remember the screened-in pool and a hot tub. I loved when we spent Easter morning at a sunrise service on the ocean. It was perfect.

Easter weekend was one of the highlights of my life. I bet my friends would not believe it. We spent one day on a pontoon boat at the mouth of the ocean; the water was so clear. Back then, we saw celebrities' houses like Burt Reynolds' home. I put baby oil on because I do not usually burn. Well, my friend from Siberia, Russia, wanted to use it and others too! I warned them to be careful. Well, that night, they went to the emergency room and was diagnosed with sun poisoning! The next day, we were on a beach and my roommate and others wore their bikinis with socks to cover up their poisoned feet. We used to do anything for a tan. I am so short. The waves would hit the back off my knee and make me fall. So there I was, minding my own business, and down I went; and I got up and went down again. I was trying to crawl and figured that would work. Then I heard, "Ma'am, are you okay?" Unfortunately he was talking to me.

There I was, with sea life in my bathing suit, trying to be cool and dragging myself along the ocean floor and said, "I'm fine, thank you." I was so embarrassed; he was on horse, cute, and I was a mess! I would travel to Florida on the weekends in college. It took about fourteen hours, and we would lay on the beach for a day. It was worth it for us, so that was nothing

Before I had disability and was a new college graduate, I found a job, got my own apartment and car. I was so proud to pay my bills and work. Working opened so many doors. I fell in love with Tim, and we traveled all over the state. I remember going camping, at the spur of the moment, with my friend Laura Kenney Napora and her husband, John. We went to Carter Caves. We all went on a three-mile hike and got lost, Tim, Laura, and I were hot and tired. There John was, with a cigarette in one hand and a beer in the other; he used to be a military guy and figured it was his survival skills.

We had a cave-crawling tour. Our leader told us it was against the law to swing at a bat (are you kidding?). If one got in my hair, I would most defiantly swing and scream. Our leader told us there was a lot of bat poop and muskrats. That was enough for me to hear, I left them all in the dust and was the first one out! I was motivated!

At night, our camp was full of skunks. We were all around the campfire and skunks came by. So I said for everyone to freeze, John and I laughed, frozen. I told them if they moved a muscle, I would kill them. The same trip, we woke up and wanted coffee, brought coffee with us, and nothing to make it in. John and I were desperate. If you drank coffee every day, like we did, you would need coffee to make sure you do not get a headache. So John and took a plastic Sprite bottle and a cup it and, took a napkin to use as a filter, and made coffee using campfire; now that was desperate! After we had to venture out and find coffee and bagels. Coffee was no problem but bagels were. Everywhere we were talking about doughnuts.

We became good friends with them and did camping on a moment's notice. One time, we went to Buckhorn, Kentucky, and we went fishing and decided to camp there. John cooked dinner on the fire. I was pregnant with Grace, in the early stages of pregnancy. I got sick and left the tent to sleep in the car. I went in the car, but I was unable to sleep due to the bullfrogs. It was their mating season, so there I was, getting sick, and I just had to get out of there. It was 3:30 a.m. and poor Tim had a sick wife and took down our tent. It made so much noise that other campers were yelling and swearing at us. They were lucky Tim is a natural peacemaker because I could have really demolished anything in my way. I remember the camp was closed and a chain was blocking our way. I was so desperate I told Tim to run over it, take it out! I was like, just do it. Tim, being the nice guy he is, woke up the guy in charge of the camp to let us out.

We could not see a thing. It was dark with drop-offs and we were in the mountains.

We did much and had a girls' night every week. We all committed to it. The girls slept over my house for a funeral and we used this time to be a girls night. It was fun, I was determined to have a girls' night. Girls, girls need girls. Boy, if we ever figured out how our lives turned out, we would find it hard to believe. We reminisced about the girls' night.

One girls' night at my house, there was spider in my carport and I did not want it to come in and make babies. The girls thought it was big too. So we got hairspray, oven cleaner, a shovel, and a bike. Tim saw that the mess we made and the spider carcass there, he knew what must have taken place. The girls' night girls would meet at everyone's house, and one night, my friend Coleen had a huge scavenger hunt. My friend and I went to hunt for roadkill—yes, it was on our list. So my friend and I said we would not get it. We went on Circle Four (Lexington, Kentucky) and somehow talked our friend to go get one and she did! We looked out the car back window and saw Laura screaming for us to open the trunk and her screaming to start the car. My friend and I laughed, and she put it in the car. We all screamed because it smelled bad. This same scavenger hunt was also to bring back a real citation from cops. So we found cops, and the police said we were scaring them and told us to park. We could get a real citation, only if we did something. I said I would do something. I told them to put on of my friend's name and information on it. We all laughed. I said to the police, "How do you scare a cop?" I then poked him in the chest and said, "Boobie." Get it? Boo bee. We all laughed. My friend was giving the police her information, and it got to her weight and we told them she was lying. It is so weird how are lives turned out.

One time, a meeting in the fall, I am in a room with many who are smart and know the Bible and they went to seminary. There is a meeting one year that I attended. Tim and I went to the hotel, a handicapped room. I was in the car, and Tim went in and was taken to a room that had a huge spider. I saw it from the parking lot, and I refused to get out of the car and go anywhere near the spider. I demanded to see the carcass of the spider and did not want it to surprise me later. Tim was able to tell I was freaking out, and he saw the spider and told the office. A lady came out with a fly swatter and knew it would not work. I think her words were, "That is big." In my head, I was like, Told ya. She went and got a guy, and he saw it was big. And I could tell it was big. He got it. I was thankful, but I was on spider alert for the time spent there.

Laura and I met through work, and we went to Cumberland Falls for a training; and in the evening, others were telling their future with bones. We were not going to do it. I do not want to know my future. I do not want to know. I noticed Laura and I were the only ones not participating. I crawled on the floor and yelled boo. She was scared and laughed. I swore she laughed, and she scared me back and we were pals from that time on. We took emotional boy clients to a haunted house that they wanted to go. So we went, and I fought to be in the middle of our group. In the back, you could sound of a chain saw. And if you're in the front, you will be scared first. It was so scary, I ran out of haunted house and left them in the dust. On the way home, Laura and I were laughing hard. And they said, "Mrs. Doubblestein and Mrs. Napora, we have never seen you like this." So funny to us.

I look back on my life and think it was fun. Even now, having a disability or being a caregiver, we look forward to our futures. Who knows what will happen to us? Our sense of humor is still with us; just because you have a disability does not mean you are so different. We can have all kinds of joy. "Very truly I tell you (Jesus is the one talking), you will weep and mourn, but the world will rejoice; you will have pain, but your pain will turn into joy" (John 16:20). I am sure St. Paul paid a huge price to follow God and got his reward in heaven. You think having a disability is bad, it could be worse.

Before I got married, I took a trip to Myrtle Beach with my friends. There was a very muscular guy wearing a girl's pink tank top and shorts. There we were, in the elevator with this guy, and we all laughed, including him. I said out loud, it was the longest elevator ride ever! We finally reached our room and got slap happy. It sounded good at the time to toss a Dixie cup of water on couples as they said good night. Well, a Dixie cup turned to an ice bucket and then a trash can. Now we did it. You could see fully where the water came from. It looked like a waterfall off our balcony. There was no denying it. Security came, and we fought over who got the door, and security told us to stop.

I do not drive anymore. When I was first paralyzed, Tim lost his job because I would pass out from low blood pressure. I felt bad. I would pass out in front of others. I am like many of you who have to rely on others. I feel like a burden to our caregivers and those who love us. I think of all my family has to put with, and I hate to relay on others. Is all this a test? I have no idea. I found a good scripture, it is, "No testing has over taken you that that is not common to everyone"(1 Corinthians 10:13).

God is faithful, and He will not let you be tested beyond your strength. But with the testing, He will provide the way out so that you may be able to endure it. God must think I am strong! My disability is permanent. What can change it? How could any of what we all go through be a test? Some things we will not know and some things are a mystery. Why do we assume we can know everything? I am the type who doesn't want to know my future. If I knew all I was going to deal with, I could not handle it. God has our best interest in mind; you have to wait on God when you have a disability. "For through the Spirit, by faith we eagerly wait for the hope of righteousness" (Galatians 5:5). Sounds desperate; we all have prayed a desperate prayer, "Lord heal me." I do, all the time.

Remember, I can only live one day at a time. Here is a popular verse, "But those who wait on the Lord shall renew their strength, they shall mount up with wings like eagles, they shall run and not be weary, they shall walk and not faint" (Isaiah 40:31). I would like to get in with that action! I would love that strength now! To have the word *no* is hard word to hear, and so many people in the Bible had it harder than I got. I was never good with the word *no*.

I was such a bad kid. I hung out at Lake St. Clair a lot. I snuck in the marinas to see all the cool boats. Harmless, right? I had to climb over barbed fence. I cut my thigh on it and was too afraid to tell my parents. Also the words *not right now*, I have never liked. I really was a kid who never let adults know what I was doing. I was a bad kid and hard to raise. The movie *Footloose* was playing all the past weekend. I snuck in when I was school age because it was real to us. Our school allowed no dancing and rock music. My mom would take my AC/DC album *Back in Black* and broke it. My parents felt backmasking on the album said smoke marijuana. She broke it, and then I said I was not going to listen to it backward, sounded wise to me. I snuck in to the movie *Footloose* by telling my parents I was going to the movie *The Natural*, starring Robert Redford.

I am a little stubborn. At times, we need to listen to our inner voice, our discernment. What of our inner voice and discernment? Mine is so wrong at times. Tim and I were picking out a couch out of my sister's home. We parked in front of house, and I walked in and asked my sister, "When did you decorate country?" A girl came out of the shower and was not my sister. I could not get words out and laughed; she knew what was going on. They had the same house and same dog.

Another time was when I took Grace to her swimming lesson and had Hope in a stroller. We had to go through the bathroom, and I was taking my girls home and went through the men's bathroom, and a guy was naked and taking a shower. I argued with a naked guy that he was in the wrong bathroom. My daughter remembered, and I was in the wrong bathroom.

I was a social worker who found social work rewarding. I always liked working, except in 2002 where I was a clinical social worker, and it was the hardest job I ever had. I was surprised to get it. I had two group interviews. I really did and acted calm but was freaking out inside. I was asked how I would handle someone who is bipolar. I named my client Bob O'Many Moods and that made all laugh. I told them I would track his mood with him and his medicine. I learned how to present a case, go before a judge, go to mental hospitals, be recorded, and had attorneys for me and against me. I swear, this is an example of good coming out of something bad. It made me a better social worker. It was so hard; I had that job offer and the same day was offered a Child Protective Services job. I lived an hour away from both and chose the clinical job.

I had the fire department and police there every day, and I had to step over the homeless people to get in the building. I felt so guilty and sad for them. For the clinical job, I had to drive an hour there and then back. My kids were still small, and Tim could work from home. I was so jealous he got the girls and I dreaded work, I really did. I had to wake up so early and get to work and see the light of my phone blinking with someone in crisis.

I learned working there, their crisis is not my crisis. You should help but not be sucked in or overwhelmed by it. I was doing clinical social work and my family would bring me lunch, and the police and fire were a daily thing there. I made them stop because Tim and I wanted to protect our kids. I fell asleep early, snuggling the kids in my bed. I was so busy at work, I had huge caseloads. I had to see people once a month and make sure their medicine were taken.

I worked with schizophrenics, bipolars, depressives, and anxiety of all kinds. I had a lady that had a borderline personality, but I was not going to put her in the hospital. It was obvious to me she wanted to. I told her I was not going to put her in the hospital, and she said she would wait until I got out of work and run me over. Sure, run me over. Of course, I was walked out with other coworkers. One time, a lady with schizoaffective disorder told me I had a white light move wherever I moved. When she told this to me, I scooted my chair over like I was moving away from the light. This made her laugh. There was a woman I was counseling who had schizophrenia. We were in a room and I asked her about her medicine; she slammed the table with her hands, and it scared me and I jumped. The panic button in the room seemed far from me and others came and waited outside my counseling room door to make sure I was okay. Her slam was loud and I ended up hospitalizing her. Do you know that when a person is needing to be hospitalized, they look different? I had a coworker tell me one time, she visited a lady in the hospital who saw the devil. She was not a Christian, she told me all about it.

I was a lucky girl though. The daughter of Aaron Beck, I think her name was Phyllis Beck, came and taught us to do cognitive therapy. My boss was a cognitive therapist and would travel to Philadelphia and bring back what she learned; and we had to use

The Structure of a Session in each appointment. I also saw Kim Burg at Fort Knox, Kentucky; she was the developer of Solution Focused Therapy, used today by many.

When I became a case social worker for those with disabilities, the paperwork was much so. I counseled a client who thought I was a little person. He would pat my head and call me a dwarf. Being able to go into their homes and knowing their caregivers and loved ones, it was good experience. I loved going to all the Chaldean's home because they always had coffee. I would help them read mail because they knew little English. There were times I needed a translator. One time, I used a translator for a client who was deaf. This was hard, the translator found me hard, because I was too fast and did not look at him. He taught me a crash course in having a deaf translator. I once called for a Chaldean client and caught a ten-dollar mistake they were just going to pay.

Little did I know, I was going to be disabled myself. Being disabled and having caregivers really opened my eyes. There is much to think about. When I was a case manager, I was close to my boss. The girl next to me had wheels on her chair. I would push her so fast, so she could not get off. I would push the chair into the boss's office and shut the door. My boss laughed, knowing that about me. It is true—I have sixth-grade boys' sense of humor.

I watch *Dr. Phil* because I like it and he is so behavioral. He uses Solution Focused Therapy and some cognitive therapy. I tell my girls all the time about people being against people, especially those who related to. I think of the last days when I watched *Dr. Phil.*

> You must understand this, that in the last days distressing times will come. For people will be lovers of themselves, lovers of money, boasters, arrogant, abusive, disobedient to their parents, ungrateful, unholy, inhuman, implacable, slanderers, profligates, brutes, haters of good, treacherous, reckless, swollen with conceit, lovers of pleasure rather than lovers of God, holding to the outward form of godliness but deny-

ing its power. Avoid them! For among them are those who make their way into households and captivate silly women, overwhelmed by their sins and swayed by all kinds of desires, who are always being instructed and can never arrive at a knowledge of the truth. As Jannes and Jambres opposed Moses, so these people, of corrupt mind and counterfeit faith, also oppose the truth. But they will not make much progress, because, as in the case of those two men their folly will become plain to everyone. Now you have observed my teaching, my conduct, my aim in life, my faith, my patience, my love, my steadfastness, my persecutions, and my suffering the things that happened to me in Antioch, Iconium, and Lystra. What persecutions I endured! Yet the Lord rescued me from all of them. Indeed, all who want to live a godly life in Christ Jesus will be persecuted. But wicked people and impostors will go from bad to worse, deceiving others and being deceived. But as for you, continue in what you have learned and firmly believed, knowing from whom you learned it, and how from childhood you have known the sacred writings that are able to instruct you for salvation through faith in Christ Jesus. All scripture is inspired by God and is useful for teaching, for reproof, for correction, and for training in righteousness, so that everyone who belongs to God may be proficient, equipped for every good work we are born with a clean slate. (2 Timothy 3)

There is no room for doubt in my life. Remember, anything that is against God is not to entertain your thoughts. Doubt came against people in the Bible. They were people with and without a disability. God's promises are for all of us. "Ask in faith, never doubting, for the one who doubts is like a wave on the sea, driven and tossed by the wind; for the doubter, being double-minded and unstable in every way, must not expect to receive anything from the Lord" (James 1:6–7).

When I was younger and not yet disabled, I was at Girl Scout camp. It was then I had my first s'more—so good! I was told if I ever got behind a horse, they would automatically kick you. No one ever said you had to spook them. It was a disaster. I was asked to put a horse away in the stall. Who tells that to a kid! I put the horse back in the stall where I was in the back of the horse. I tried to be quiet and began to cry because I did not know what to do. Some adult heard me crying and told me I had to spook the horse. Oh, just when I was feeling comfortable again around animals, I saw a bull tied up and figured, no he cannot hurt me, not so much. I was going to feed the bull an apple. I dropped it, and we both decided to pick it up at the same time. He hit my head with the horn so hard, and I was now bleeding! No stiches were needed.

In college, I had to do a genealogy on my family, both sides of the family. My mother was the oldest of twelve and my dad was the oldest of seven. I had big Sicilian family and, I think, about thirty-four first cousins alone. I was allowed to do my dad's side; after great profanities, I did it.

My first car was a beat-up Subaru that you could see the road from the bottom. Some others remember the car. One time, my friend and I drove it to a ride in the country and a turkey vulture went for some roadkill on the road. It flew for it right in front of our car, and its wingspan covered my window and we screamed and laughed; we were surprised. The car backfired like Uncle Buck's car in the movie called *Uncle Buck*. I had bought it for $300, and it was a stick. I learned on Kentucky hills! One time, I got it stuck on a hill and it kept on stalling on me. A guy moved it and got it started. I was getting yelled at and sworn at. I was embarrassed but survived. It was hard for me to drive. I stupidly had it fixed so much; it was not worth having and the bang of the backfire would scare all. I thought it was funny

I went to college at Asbury University in Wilmore, Kentucky. My friends and I would hike at Lock 7, the high-bridge area. Now they have guardrails and a park there. I remember hiking a lot and we hiked near Shakertown. I did a lot of hiking with my friends. We hiked at the Kentucky River and Shakertown. One time, we went hiking and my friend lost her shoe in the mud. Priceless! I can see it now. We went off the path, the only way out was for us to go up. It was so steep, and we had to lay our bodies against the hill. We did, and I saw crawly things like spiders and centipedes. I did not like what I saw and was the first one up, knocking a log down after them! They put up with me. We bonded together; others would think we were sisters. At that time, it was a small campus and we were the only one besides the New Jersey group who had dark hair. Big blond hair and dollies as collars were in.

In junior year of college, I lived in a house with my friends. I remember my friend and I would tear up a room to get rid of a cave cricket. Look it up and you will see why. One day, we trapped a huge spider in a bathroom, under a see-through jar. I warned all and told them to use the other bathroom and if anyone dumped over the jar, they would be dead ducks. I heard a scream, a jar, and then a laugh. It was my friend! I was going to kill her! I was not able to make her a dead duck because she kept on laughing. The girl was a good friend to me, and I could always find something funny out of someone's misfortune. This is not always a good thing! My good friend and I stayed friends. She got bitten on the butt by a dog and needed stitches! This was bad and funny to me at the same time. I could see her in the emergency, saying, "A dog bit me in the butt! You can imagine what the doctor must have thought. I can see the doctor talking to his buddies about this. See, with me having a disability, I was embarrassed all the time. It was her turn now.

Now there was a time my sister went to the same college and kidded around like I did. She put my mattress on the bathroom stalls. Classic! The funniest thing she ever did was place Saran Wrap tightly over the toilet seats on my floor! It had her written all over it. I knew she had to be involved. I had fun in college, my sister and I like humor. We can just look at each other and know what the other is thinking. I could always count on my friend. I taught her sister how to drive and her too.

I had to move back to my parents home. My dad acknowledged I was sad and missed Kentucky, and he would play cards and have Chinese food. I like he acknowledged my sadness. As a result, my friend picked me up from Michigan to Kentucky. I had only $100 to go back on and knew I would end up in Kentucky. I could always count on my friend. I taught her sister how to drive and her too.

This was too funny! My friend just got her license and she was driving back to Wilmore from Nicholasville (about twenty minutes), and there were some kids riding on the road. I stuck out my fist to them and said, "Hey, you kids, get out of the road, this is no cross-walk." As soon as I said it, we laughed because I was so serious about it. Poor friend, she had to drive back while we had a laugh attack.

I worked through college. I must tell you about a time I was working with a friend at a Japanese restaurant. Let me say, rice is hard to get out of carpet and we worked at 2:00 a.m. to clean it. There was a basement and drywall that was shaped like a person shoved in it and tons of blood on it. I looked at my friend, and we were both freaked out. They told us to dust and not say a word about what we saw. We stupidly said okay. We went to the basement to dust and saw a VIP video room. I told my friend I was not going in there. They had some illegal gambling going on in that room. We decided to dust a chess-like game that had four players. We started to dust it and the game they were playing went down and a new game popped up. I screamed, "What did we do!" We knew it was bad, so we ran and never went back or got paid. I told her after that night, I was never coming back no matter how much they played.

I had to move back to my parents for a few months during college to save money.

College was fun. My friends and I wore all black and drew facial hair and dropped rice on couples when they said good night. This was long before the college put in an elevator and a window was looking down on couple. I now know that was not the best idea. I also, took the clothes of other student as they were showering and they used the shower curtain to cover up.

Later before disability, I had a twisted bowel and a growth of scar tissue. I thought I was dying and no one was telling me a thing.

I asked why all the fish were here and thought I was at a pizza party. The fish were all my relatives and I saw them most at parties. It took a long recovery. I thought I would never get better and cried to my in-laws. I had an open wound, poor Tim had to pack for me each day. I also had a feeding tube. I saw my doctor come and sit on a chair in my room, praying. He thought I was sleeping and saying he was so sorry. I believed him.

My cousin came over at the home and went to feed me with the stomach tube, and stomach juices went into her mouth. I could see her face and the horror she felt. I heard her on the phone to her sister about the horror she felt. I had to sleep sitting up. And I was praying one night to God, I could not go through another day hurting anymore and needed Him to do something; I was desperate. I woke up the next morning feeling better. Recovery takes so long. God must have known and heard my prayer.

We all have times in our lives times when we had our prayers answered and unanswered. No one wants to talk about unanswered prayers. We can mark times of our lives where we knew God must have done something. I can think of many like graduating college, marrying Tim, having kids, and getting Lilly, our dog. In the Bible, people would make an altar at places God intervened.

> Noah built an alter to the Lord, and took of every clean bird, and burnt offerings on the alter. (Genesis 8:20)

> So Abraham moved his tent, and came and settled by the Oaks of Mamre, which are at Hebron; and there he built an altar. (Genesis 13:18)

There are many verses about altars being built. You can use the Bible concordance. We do this mentally. I am person with a disability. There are days I may feel alone, but I am not alone. I have had a good life, and my future will be no different. When you have a disability does not mean God is done with us. God is not done with anyone.

CHAPTER 10

I like television and I like to watch a cooking show named *Chopped*. Now it is important to not put your faith in others but in God; people are all mortals and will fail you. These days, we have Facebook. We never grew up with this; likes and followings on Facebook seems so important to others so blocking is a big deal. I blocked a person and got blocked and just do not think about it. I blocked someone for Hope. I said to Hope, whose head is on the chopping board, "I chopped (blocked) this person."

I know laughter is medicine. WebMD says the following about laughter:

Laughter's Effects on the Body

In the last few decades, researchers have studied laughter's effects on the body and turned up some potentially interesting information on how it affects us:

- Blood flow Researchers at the University of Maryland studied the effects on blood vessels when people were shown either comedies or dramas. After the screening, the blood vessels of the group who watched the comedy behaved normally—expanding and contracting easily. But the blood vessels in people who watched the drama tended to tense up, restricting blood flow.

- Immune response. Increased stress is associated with decreased immune system response, says Provide some studies have shown that the ability to use humor may raise the level of infection-fighting antibodies in the body and boost the levels of immune cells, as well.
- Blood sugar levels. One study of 19 people with diabetes looked at the effects of laughter on blood sugar levels. After eating, the group attended a tedious lecture. On the next day, the group ate the same meal and then watched a comedy. After the comedy, the group had lower blood sugar levels than they did after the lecture.

Relaxation and sleep. The focus on the benefits of laughter really began with Norman Cousin's memoir, *Anatomy of an Illness*. Cousins, who was diagnosed with ankylosing spondylitis, a painful spine condition, found that a diet of comedies, like Marx Brothers films and episodes of Candid Camera, helped him feel better. He said that ten minutes of laughter allowed him two hours of pain-free sleep.

The Evidence: Is Laughter the Best Medicine?

But things get murky when researchers try to sort out the full effects of laughter on our minds and bodies. Is laughter really good for you? Can it actually boost your energy? Not everyone is convinced.

"I don't mean to sound like a curmudgeon," says Provine, "but the evidence that laughter has health benefits is iffy at best."

He says that most studies of laughter have been small and not well-conducted. He also says too many researchers have an obvious bias: they go into the study wanting to prove that laughter has benefits.

Last night, Tim and I had a laugh attack. I am unable to laugh, I cry and make a noise. For me, I had my blood drop, not rise. I could not get my laugh out. I had not laughed right since I have been paralyzed; it feels like my laugh box is frozen. I told Tim I lied to a priest at my first confession before I had my First Communion. It tickled us. Tim said that our lives were based on a lie. I thought it was so funny and a funny thing he said. I must tell you, I would laugh at my poor kids' expense. I would jump out of nowhere, yell, "*Boo*" at them and they would be so mad at me, with good reason. Now, I wait till they are quiet, and if they are even kissing—bonus. I enjoy scaring them, and their significant others would be surprised. They look up and my kids say, "Aww, Mom. Really." Their boyfriends look up and have a look of shock and fear in their eyes. It does not help my chair makes noise and I can't get out my laugh. What is a girl to do? I get my husband involved in scaring them, that is what I do. I love the funny stuff.

Now I must tell you two true funny stories. I had some friends drive her dad's car and they went to pick up someone. In the car, a M-80 went off in the back seat of the car. They all bailed but the car was still moving. The back seat of the car was ruined and so they never told anyone, including the dad. They had to hide the car and fix it with a new seat, they did. I love that story. They know who they are, and the next story happened to them. They snuck out at night and went to the Shelter. The one featured in the movie *8 Mile*. I went with them to there and the Garden Bowl in Detroit it was uneventful. It is hard to believe. So the girls in the last story went to the Shelter and ended up getting in an accident on the way back; they ran into a guard wall on the freeway. The bouncer at the club helped them out, and the parents never knew that story. I will not say who it is out of respect for the parent who are still alive.

I stayed over at summer in college. We worked and stayed in the dorm for free. We ran the dorm like a hotel. I had my weekends free. I was getting ready for a date and went outside for something. Shoulder pads were in, and I adjusted mine. I somehow got a wasp in my shirt and I looked like I was doing the Lambada SP and it stung me, of course. I ran into the dorm bathroom, getting more stings, and took of my shirt and the wasp was on the floor. I was so mad about it stinging me right before I had a date. I took some Benadryl since I was stung a lot. The guy I had a date with helped me move one time, and he got trapped in a room with a bumblebee and screamed. I laughed so much, I am sure this made him mad and I never got asked out again.

In college, I laughed so much. I went to college at Asbury in Kentucky. I lived part of the time in Glide Crawford Dorm, third floor. That is still called Third Herd. It got that name from sounding like a herd of buffalo being heard. College was some of the best times of my life. We decided to sled on Kentucky hills by getting a plastic paint tarp form the town hardware store for free. You could sled with ten other people down a hill fast. Now that was fun! Those who attended Asbury College or Seminary remember the plastic cups we used in the cafeteria. Remember, the loud sound they made when they fell off a tray? I thought that was so great, I decided it was funny to knock them off my friend's tray and make that loud noise that would get everyone to look. I had a friend and I would knock down her cups on the floor; everyone stared at her.

I was found out and got it happened to me, so I bowed and proceeded to knock down my friend's cup. I later made the dorm floor play the game called blind's man bluff as adults. We played in the Glide Crawford basement, turned off the lights, pitch-black, and we had to freeze and the person who was it had to find us.

We never crossed the street where Asbury Seminary was in fear we would fall in love with a pastor and be a pastor's wife. There was a saying, "Glide Crawford girls get a Mrs. Diploma." God must have a sense of humor because I fell in love with a pastor who got his master's at Asbury Seminary. He was also from Michigan. For all my trying, I ended up marrying him.

I like to visit a cousin and I was ready for bed and was dropped mistakenly. Tim was upset and he called my cousin for help, and I said, "I have fallen and can't get up." To us, we had a laugh attack and I was not hurt at all. She made it funny like me. I saw at that time how she responded. I do not like to be vulnerable, and I saw she does not too.

I had had a good fun life and will continue to have more fun in life, being disabled. My sister came to Kentucky from Michigan and we, with some of my friends, decided to spend the day and night at the Kentucky River at Lock 7. We made a fire and barbecued, swam, and fished. I used some minnows for bait and was catching fish. I was so excited and showed all. Then, on a boat, coming straight for us was the Department of Animals. At the time, I did not know who they were. I proudly showed off, making sure they saw my fish. I was fishing without a license. I almost got off of having a ticket until one guy on the boat told the others on the boat this was how they get paid a salary. Suddenly their demeanor changed and I had at ticket for fishing without a license for seventy-five dollars. I had to pay it myself. We had a good time until night. We decided to sleep by the river without any shelter, not even a tent. Night came, and the fire did keep us warm. The person my sister brought was chopping down a tree with his bare hands. We were so cold and lying on the rocks did not help. No thought of danger came to us like copperhead snakes. We just did it, we paid no attention to the dangers. We were so happy when morning came.

CHAPTER 11

It is so hard to love your enemies. We are called to.

> But I say to you listen, love your enemies, do good to those who hate you, bless those who hurt curse you. Pray for those that abuse you. If anyone strikes you on the cheek, offer the other also; and from anyone who takes your coat do not even hold your shirt. Give to everyone who begs from you; and if anyone takes away your goods do not ask for them again. Do to others what you would have them to do to you. If you love those who love you. What credit is that to you? For even sinners love those who love them. If you do good to those who do good to you what credit is that to you? For even sinners do the same. If you lend to those from whom you hope to receive, what credit is that to you? Even sinners lend to sinners, to receive as much again. But love your enemies, do good, and lend, expecting nothing in return. Your reward will be great, and you will be children of the Highest; for he is kind to the ungrateful and the wicked. Be merciful, just as your Father is merciful. (Luke 6:27–36)

How hard to not be nice to those you do not like. It is rude to throw a Xanax in someone's mouth when they are talking. I remember an episode of *Seinfeld* where Elaine was talking to another and nodding her head yes but, in her head, was talking to herself, saying, *Shut up, stop talking.* There are times I think like this.

There was a time where we ran a dorm in college like a hotel. I spent my summers working on the cleanup crew and did not like a girl I was working with at all. She drove me nuts! She was mean, and I could not believe she acted mean and did not realize it. I prayed and complained to God and prayed five good things to happen for her. Her behavior got worse! I just kept on praying and we got into a fight. The flesh in me was not going to have it, so she went into a bathroom stall and I went in, kicked the door open, and raised my fist to her and was getting ready to hit her. Just as I was getting to hit her, I saw her fear and felt bad; the bad feeling washed all over me. I went to a broom closet and argued with God about not apologizing—I lost. I went to her and said sorry, I treated her well after that. I bought her lunch and continued to pray; we became friends.

I know this will work for you most of the time. Let me tell you about a time it did not end in a friendship. I received a phone call from someone I thought was a friend. She called me inconsiderate. I let her have it big-time! Tim sat on the couch and could not believe me talking that way; I was so mean. They were moving up in the church and talked bad about us. I can handle not being liked, but Tim is nice and a peacemaker. I knew they were wrong and I let her have it. I knew we were talked bad about, and they were so moved up in the church. I did not to say a bad word about them as they were acting bad. Again. I was convicted by God. Darn it! I prayed and brought them stuff; I was to act like they were not my enemy. God loved them too; that God loved them helped me to forgive and I did not think of them until I wrote this book. I have a huge temper, and when I am convicted, I know. They ended up not liking my family and blocked me on Facebook.

I got lucky because they moved away. I chalked it up as their loss because I felt we were fabulous! We have lot of friends and family. Do you know 10 percent of people will not like you. I think I saw this somewhere. They probably do not think about you as much as you think they do. I have always told my family that for everyone who do not like who you are, there are at least three that do like you.

What is really on my mind and cannot shake is what God thinks of us right now, with a disability or more. We are not lesser children of God, nor does he love us less. We might feel this especially if we have a disability. Believe or not, while we are in our mortal broken bodies, God still gives us stuff as we wait till His Second Coming.

One of the biggest things is forgiveness for our sins. How about forgiveness for our sin? "If we confess our sins, he who is faithful and just will forgive us our sins and cleanse us from all unrighteousness. If we say that we have not sinned, we make him a liar, and His word is not in us. Right now, as we are He forgives us. So, we get forgiveness" (1 John 1:9–10).

He will get the promise right now. He will not test us and will provide a way out. "No testing has overtaken you that is not common to everyone" (1 Corinthians 10:13). God is faithful, and He will not let you be tested beyond your strength; but with the testing, He will also provide the way out so that you may be able to endure it. I can hear you now, "My disability is not going away." He must think you can deal with disabilities.

We get sins forgiven and a way out of tests. Here is what else. "Peter said to them, 'Repent, and be baptized every one of you in the name of Jesus Christ so that your sins may be forgiven; and you will receive the gift of the Holy Spirit. For the promise is for you, for your children, and for all who are far away, everyone whom the Lord our God calls to him" (Acts 2:38–39).

Not bad the promise of the Holy Spirit. "Trust in the Lord, and do good; so you will live in the land, and enjoy security. Take delight in the Lord, he will give you the desires of your heart" (Psalms 37:3–4). King David wrote this about God. He was a king and related to Jesus, and God walked with him and he made mistakes. He did what was right before God. "Nevertheless for David's sake the Lord his God gave him a lamp in Jerusalem, setting up his son after him, and establishing Jerusalem; because David did what was right in the sight of the Lord" (1 Kings 15:4). He had made trouble for himself; nevertheless, he struggled with sin like us. He committed murder and fornication. You may feel like you do bad things, God will still have you if you repent and try to not do the same sin. You try, God will help you be "Right in His sight."

> For thus says the Lord: Only when Babylon's seventy years are completed will I visit you, and I will fulfill to you my promise and bring you back to this place. For surely I know the plans I have for you, says the Lord, plans for your welfare and not for harm, to give you a future with hope. Then when you call upon me and come and pray to me, I will hear you. When you search for me, you will find me; if you seek me with all your heart, I will let you find me, says the Lord, and I will restore your fortunes and gather you from all the nations and all the places where I have driven you, says the Lord, and I will bring you back to the place from which I sent you into exile. (Jeremiah 29:10–14)

What sticks out for me is the word *hope*. Things were bad for the Israelites; they were taken by the Babylonians for a long time. We may feel our bad times and disability is bad and have no hope. This was said for the Israelites. God hears our prayers, and nothing surprises Him. He gives us hope, being disabled.

I do not like any kind of discipline. It is hard to give discipline and be the one to receive it.

> Endure trials for the sake of discipline. God is treating as children for what child is there whom a parent does not discipline? If you do not have that discipline in which all children share, then you are illegitimate and not his children. Moreover, we had human parents to discipline us, and we respected them. Should we not be even more willing to be subject to the Father of Spirits and live? For they disciplined us for a short time

as seemed best to them, but He disciplined us for our good, in order that we may share in His holiness. Now, discipline always seems painful rather than pleasant at the time, but later yields the peaceful fruit of righteousness to those who have been trained in it. (Hebrews 12:7–11)

My child, do not despise the Lords discipline or be weary of His reproof, for the Lord reproves the one He loves, as a father the son whom he delights. (Proverbs 3:11–12)

How happy is the one whom God reproves; therefore, do not despise the discipline of the Almighty. He knows what beat He know better than we do. (Job 5:17)

But you, O Lord, know me' you see me and test me me-my heart is with You. Pull them out like sheep for the slaughter and set them apart for the day of the slaughter. (Jeremiah 12:3)

We are called to be humbled. This explains it better: the parable of the Pharisee and the tax collector:

He also told this parable to some who trusted in themselves that they were righteous and regarded others with contempt: "Two men went up to the temple to pray, one a Pharisee and the other a tax collector. The Pharisee, standing by himself, was praying thus, 'God, I thank you that I am not like other people: thieves, rogues, adulterers, or even like this tax collector. I fast twice a week; I give a tenth of all my income.' But the tax collector, standing far off, would not even look up to heaven, but was beating his breast and saying,

'God, be merciful to me, a sinner!' I tell you, this man went down to his home justified rather than the other; for all who exalt themselves will be humbled, but all who humble themselves will be exalted." (Luke 18:9–14)

You know that in the book of Luke, to be exalted and humbled is used more than one time.

When he noticed how the guests chose the places of honor, he told them a parable. "When you are invited by someone to a wedding banquet, do not sit down at the place of honor, in case someone more distinguished than you has been invited by your host; and the host who invited both of you may come and say to you, 'Give this person your place,' and then in disgrace you would start to take the lowest place. But when you are invited, go and sit down at the lowest place, so that when your host comes, he may say to you, 'Friend, move up higher'; then you will be honored in the presence of all who sit at the table with you. For all who exalt themselves will be humbled, and those who humble themselves will be exalted." (Luke 13:7-11)

It must be important to be told by Jesus two times in the same book.

I want to tell you a true story about my family that they remember. My girls had bunk beds and I was on the top, making them up. I saw out of the corner of my eye, my youngest, Hope, sliding down her dad's car and saying, "*Weeee*." I could not get words out and sounded like the dad on *A Christmas Story*, trying to fix the furnace. The kids came from the neighborhood and were taking turns sliding down Tim's car with the hose of water.

Tim came running and asked me what was wrong. I could only point and say, "Look!" I could not believe what they were doing, having a good time. We gave them something else to do and did not punish them because we felt that did not warrant a punishment; they were looking for fun. My aunt had a wooden spoon, and we had to sign it after we were punished. I was so proud my name was not on it. My cousin and I were in her sister's room and we put a mattress on the floor and went to her top bunk. We thought that was good fun. She and I would take turns swinging onto the ceiling light and falling back on the bed mattress. Her dad came to check on us, and there was my cousin, on the light, yelling, "*Wee.*" She was hanging on the ceiling light. There was no way out, she was caught.

Now there was a time I had to punish my youngest. She took my liquid eyeliner and, with her friend, painted a tree. I loved my makeup and was upset about it and grounded her to her room. She hated that and used to throw herself down like she had no bones. I was blessed my girls took their punishments. It was not easy, and they were so cute. I think God made them cute so we would not kill them!

One time, Tim was watching them and working on the computer and the girls got to a red velvet cake. When I got home, they were covered in it. I asked them if they had any cake, and they said, "No, Mommy." Clearly they had. They were too funny with that cake all over their faces.

One more funny story. I had Hope on my hip and talking to my cousin on the phone and thought Hope fell asleep. I think I carried her everywhere and thought nothing of it. She was eating a chocolate cake I made and when I looked at her, she said, "Yummy." I hang on to the words my mother-in-law told me, "Out of all the mothers of the world, I was chosen to be theirs." She does not remember that, I do.

When Hope was to be born, Grace, her older sister, said, "Yeah, Grandma and Grandpa are coming!" She could not wait to see them. I was in labor and all she could think of were her grandparents. Hope was born, and Grace thought of her as a minion. She was in heaven and could make Hope laugh. One time, they were too quiet and I thought they were up to something. There Grace was, feeding her licks of her lollipop. I knew something was up.

I followed all my parents' house rules because if my dad yelled, you could feel it in your belly! I was a kid who got spanked and would tell him, "That doesn't hurt." I felt it, and it hurt. If my dad said, "Not another peep," I had to get the last word and I would say, "Peep." There was a time I was older and dated a guy and we went to Bobo Island and out to eat later. I swear I had permission, I would not just disobey like that; I was too chicken of making my dad mad. When I was dropped off at the wee hours, the lights to my house were on; I knew I was in big trouble. I told my boyfriend to not walk me to the door. My parents were mad, even had my sister see if I was at my cousin's house to see if I was there. In their eyes, I could be hurt and I disobeyed them. They said they were about to call the police. That would freak me out. I realize now, with time, I was really a kid that hid so much.

I had a childhood male friend; we were just friends. We lived on the same street and were each other's date for homecomings and proms. We knew each other since we were little and went to the same elementary school. We hung out a lot, we spent the time out laughing. Back then, we were 1970s kids. Back then, we were told to come home when the streetlights came on. We rode our bikes to the St. Clair Lake, near Lakeshore Drive. You have to grow up in St. Clair Shores to get it.

I was so bad. We rode our bikes, and the fish flies were out. If you live near the water, you know what they are. Look at St. Clair Shores fish flies and see, they look like a plague and even needed the street cleaners to clean the streets. It caused so many accidents. They covered everything: doors, shop windows, it felt like they were everywhere. I got used to them. My friend and I were riding bikes next to each other and I pushed him in a bush, and all I could see was one tire of his bike and fish flies everywhere and his scream. I remember we would both stop suddenly and try to make us fall. I ended up in a truck, off my bike, which fell. At Lake Shore Drive, we would watch the barges go by Lake St. Clair and other people would walk by and we would say something embarrassing like, "I am keeping my baby!"

or "You forgot our anniversary." We had so much fun hanging out and had many laugh attacks. We said we were going to see a movie and went to parties. Since he was driving and we were not big drinkers, we held the same beer cup and pretended to drink.

It would not be fun when others that I do not know would ask me what happened or others in public would want to heal me for their glory. I came to the point of not allowing others to pray for me in public. I would tell them my name and tell them they could pray privately for me. People would say comments, all the time, they would never make to anyone else. I would be nice and embarrassed at the same time. I don't get the fight or flight response. I would get ready to fight privately.

I have like a tunnel vision to be in the right standing in God's eye. I think those of us who have a disability or more than one has a different experience than others, not any better or worse, just different. I always say that life never goes as planned. I am a schedule-and-list girl as always. Having a disability, we can think it is not fair. I am so guilty of this and no way ready to deal with this until now. I guess God thinks I can handle this. I beg God to not have to handle stuff, it is mostly uncomfortable and embarrassing for me. Stay with me here, we *have* to deal with a disability and being a Christian; knowing we are a child of God, why on earth are we not healed physically? See, those of us who have a physical disability want to be physically healed and do not think about the soul being healed as much.

I keep on thinking how Moses prayed for the Israelites, even they talked smack about him many times. Talk about forgiveness. I would want to stick it to them and use the fact I had a powerful buddy (God). He seemed to pray for them no matter what, even when he was being talked bad about.

> From Mount Hor they set out by the way to the Red Sea, to go around the land of Edom; but the people became impatient on the way. The people spoke against God and against Moses, "Why have you brought us up out of Egypt to die in the wilderness? For there is no food and no water,

and we detest this miserable food." Then the Lord sent poisonous serpents among the people, and they bit the people, so that many Israelites died. The people came to Moses and said, "We have sinned by speaking against the Lord and against you; pray to the Lord to take away the serpents from us." So, Moses prayed for the people. And the Lord said to Moses, "Make a poisonous serpent, and set it on a pole; and everyone who is bitten shall look at it and live." So Moses made a serpent of bronze, and put it upon a pole; and whenever a serpent bit someone, that person would look at the serpent of bronze and live. (Numbers 21:4–9)

Don't you wish you can look at a serpent and be healed of your disability?

Why is it never talked about or ever seen in the movies about Moses's hand, withered up at the time he was called by God?

Again, the Lord said to him, "Put your hand inside your cloak." He put his hand into his cloak; and when he took it out, his hand was leprous, as white as snow. Then God said, "Put your hand back into your cloak"—so he put his hand back into his cloak, and when he took it out, it was restored like the rest of his body. (Exodus 4:6–7)

You may say, "If God has the power hold healing, why am I not healed like Moses got healed?" I guess we will not know why we are not healed. I want God on my side. Not being healed is bad and hard to deal with, I need God to live this life.

I feel the Israelites have a bad rap with the golden calf and all. They had seen a pillar of fire and a cloud; you would think this would have them tap into God's divine intervention. I think they must have gotten so used to it, easy to do. Today we struggle with the exact same thing—what about when we see rainbows? I am guilty and think they are pretty and forget this was a sign.

> Then God said to Noah and to his sons with him, "As for me, I am establishing my covenant with you and your descendants after you, and with every living creature that is with you, the birds, the domestic animals, and every animal of the earth with you, as many as came out of the ark. I establish my covenant with you, that never again shall all flesh be cut off by the waters of a flood, and never again shall there be a flood to destroy the earth." God said, "This is the sign of the covenant that I make between me and you and every living creature that is with you, for all future generations: I have set my bow in the clouds, and it shall be a sign of the covenant between me and the earth. When I bring clouds over the earth and the bow is seen in the clouds, I will remember my covenant that is between me and you and every living creature of all flesh; and the waters shall never again become a flood to destroy all flesh. When the bow is in the clouds, I will see it and remember the everlasting covenant between God and every living creature of all flesh that is on the earth." God said to Noah, "This is the sign of the covenant that I have established between me and all flesh that is on the earth." (Genesis 9:8–17)

See? There are scientific facts about rainbows, I choose to ignore them because it was a sign of a covenant first before there was scientifics.

Paul and Silas had to ultimately show forgiveness; look at the following scriptures:

> One day, as we were going to the place of prayer, we met a slave-girl who had a spirit of divination and brought her owners a great deal of money by fortune-telling. While she followed Paul and us, she would cry out, "These men are slaves of the Most High God, who proclaim to you a way of salvation." She kept doing this for many days. But Paul, very much annoyed, turned and said to the spirit, "I order you in the name of Jesus Christ to come out of her." And it came out that very hour.
>
> But when her owners saw that their hope of making money was gone, they seized Paul and Silas and dragged them into the marketplace before the authorities. When they had brought them before the magistrates, they said, "These men are disturbing our city; they are Jews and are advocating customs that are not lawful for us as Romans to adopt or observe." The crowd joined in attacking them, and the magistrates had them stripped of their clothing and ordered them to be beaten with rods. After they had given them a severe flogging, they threw them into prison and ordered the jailer to keep them securely. Following these instructions, he put them in the innermost cell and fastened their feet in the stocks.
>
> About midnight Paul and Silas were praying and singing hymns to God, and the prisoners were listening to them. Suddenly there was an earthquake, so violent that the foundations of the prison were shaken; and immediately all the doors were opened and everyone's chains were unfastened. When the jailer woke up and saw the

prison doors wide open, he drew his sword and was about to kill himself, since he supposed that the prisoners had escaped. But Paul shouted in a loud voice, "Do not harm yourself, for we are all here." The jailer called for lights, and rushing in, he fell down trembling before Paul and Silas. Then he brought them outside and said, "Sirs, what must I do to be saved?" They answered, "Believe on the Lord Jesus, and you will be saved, you and your household." They spoke the word of the Lord to him and to all who were in his house. At the same hour of the night he took them and washed their wounds; then he and his entire family were baptized without delay. He brought them up into the house and set food before them; and he and his entire household rejoiced that he had become a believer in God.

When morning came, the magistrates sent the police, saying, "Let those men go." And the jailer reported the message to Paul, saying, "The magistrates sent word to let you go; therefore come out now and go in peace." But Paul replied, "They have beaten us in public, uncondemned, men who are Roman citizens, and have thrown us into prison; and now are they going to discharge us in secret? Certainly not! Let them come and take us out themselves." The police reported these words to the magistrates, and they were afraid when they heard that they were Roman citizens; so they came and apologized to them. And they took them out and asked them to leave the city. After leaving the prison they went to Lydia's home; and when they had seen and encouraged the brothers and sisters there, they departed. (Acts 16:16–40)

You know what stands out to me? They were accused wrongly, flogged, and thrown in prison. Talk about the ultimate forgiveness. I would want to stick it to them, make them all pay for all the wrong, especially the flogging.

We are supposed to have the fruit of the Spirit. Have you ever heard the phrase, "I like people, but Christians I don't like?" That is a popular phrase, and it has some truth to it; wonder why?" We must live by the Spirit of God Look at Galatians 5:16–21:

> Live by the Spirit, I say, and do not gratify the desires of the flesh. For what the flesh desires is opposed to the Spirit, and what the Spirit desires is opposed to the flesh; for these are opposed to each other, to prevent you from doing what you want. But if you are led by the Spirit, you are not subject to the law. Now the works of the flesh are obvious: fornication, impurity, licentiousness, idolatry, sorcery, enmities, strife, jealousy, anger, quarrels, dissensions, factions, envy, drunkenness, carousing, and things like these. I am warning you, as I warned you before: those who do such things will not inherit the kingdom of God.

Guilty of some? I know I am guilty of some and must practice to not have them. The fruit of the Spirit are:

> By contrast, the fruit of the Spirit is love, joy, peace, patience, kindness, generosity, faithfulness, gentleness, and self-control. There is no law against such things. And those who belong to Christ Jesus have crucified the flesh with its passions and desires. If we live by the Spirit, let us also be guided by the Spirit. Let us not become conceited, competing against one another, envying one another. (Galatians 5:22–26)

Look at the parable of the prodigal son. Here it is to jog your memory.

> Then Jesus said, "There was a man who had two sons. The younger of them said to his father, 'Father, give me the share of the property that will belong to me.' So he divided his property between them. A few days later the younger son gathered all he had and traveled to a distant country, and there he squandered his property in dissolute living. When he had spent everything, a severe famine took place throughout that country, and he began to be in need. So he went and hired himself out to one of the citizens of that country, who sent him to his fields to feed the pigs. He would gladly have filled himself with the pods that the pigs were eating; and no one gave him anything. But when he came to himself he said, 'How many of my father's hired hands have bread enough and to spare, but here I am dying of hunger! I will get up and go to my father, and I will say to him, "Father, I have sinned against heaven and before you; I am no longer worthy to be called your son; treat me like one of your hired hands."' So he set off and went to his father. But while he was still far off, his father saw him and was filled with compassion; he ran and put his arms around him and kissed him. Then the son said to him, 'Father, I have sinned against heaven and before you; I am no longer worthy to be called your son.' But the father said to his slaves, 'Quickly, bring out a robe—the best one—and put it on him; put a ring on his finger and sandals on his feet. And get the fatted calf and kill it and let us eat and celebrate; for this son of mine was

dead and is alive again; he was lost and is found!'
And they began to celebrate.

"Now his elder son was in the field; and
when he came and approached the house, he
heard music and dancing. He called one of the
slaves and asked what was going on. He replied,
'Your brother has come, and your father has killed
the fatted calf, because he has got him back safe
and sound.' Then he became angry and refused
to go in. His father came out and began to plead
with him. But he answered his father, 'Listen! For
all these years I have been working like a slave for
you, and I have never disobeyed your command;
yet you have never given me even a young goat so
that I might celebrate with my friends. But when
this son of yours came back, who has devoured
your property with prostitutes, you killed the
fatted calf for him!' Then the father said to him,
'Son, you are always with me, and all that is mine
is yours. But we had to celebrate and rejoice,
because this brother of yours was dead and has
come to life; he was lost and has been found.'"
(Luke 15:11–32)

Don't you feel the older son was right? The older son followed
all the rules, never disobeyed his father. I would be angry too and
feel the same. I just cannot be the only one. I felt, for a long time,
my disabilities were hard and I followed all God's rules. I followed
all God's rules and still had disabilities. Disability is not fair; we can
be stuck with them. Life sure is not fair, and we go through hard and
easy times. Remember, life never goes as planned.

God can do anything right? Nothing is impossible with God.
An angel told this to Mary, "'For nothing will be impossible with
God.' Then Mary said, 'Here am I, the servant of the Lord; let it be
with me according to your word.' Then the angel departed from her"
(Luke 1:37–38).

If nothing is impossible for God, why do we have disabilities? I tell you personally, to have this hard disability, I had a different reliance of God than if I had not had if I had no disabilities. Remember, His ways are not ours and He can see our whole lives and around corners.

ABOUT THE AUTHOR

Anna Doubblestein is a forty-nine-year-old wife, mother, and social worker. In 2008, she experienced a year of crisis beginning with the death of her father, grandmother, and godmother. Following a spinal surgery in December of that year, she found herself paralyzed. Battles with addiction to pain medications, loss of a career she loved, and other difficulties, while trying to hold on to her faith in God, left her with a unique insight to His love. Anna has been married to her husband, Tim, for twenty-four years. She has two daughters and one very cute dog. She loves living in Northeastern Michigan on Lake Huron.

CPSIA information can be obtained
at www.ICGtesting.com
Printed in the USA
LVHW110840070720
659732LV00004BA/208

9 781098 036997